Sporting Volkswagens

A freelance motoring writer and a past assistant editor of *VW Motoring* magazine, Laurence Meredith is a Volkswagen enthusiast and Beetle owner of many years standing. His professional interests include all types of classic cars and to that end, has contributed to a number of publications including *Classic Car Weekly, VolksWorld, Classic Cars, AutoClassic and Popular Classics* in addition to regional newspapers.

Laurence has competed in a number of events over the years including MCC Trials and historic rallies but, in his words, prefers to "record the insanities of the world with a camera and a word processor rather than participate in them".

His is also the author of 'The Original VW Beetle' published by Bay View Books of Devon and is soon to embark on his third book, 'The Original Porsche 356'.

Sporting Volkswagens

by

Laurence Meredith

BREWIN BOOKS

First published
by Brewin Books, Studley, Warwickshire, B80 7LG
in March 1994

ISBN 1 85858 027 7

British Library Cataloguing in Publication Data.
A Catalogue record for this book is available from the British Library

Typeset in Times by Avon Dataset, Bidford on Avon, Warwickshire, B50 4JH
and made and printed by The Cromwell Press, Melksham, Wiltshire, SN12 8PH.

Acknowledgements

I am indebted to the following people for supplying facts, figures and photographs for this book; George Shetliffe, John Maher, Bob Beales, Dennis Greenslade, Mike Hinde, Bill Bengry, Laurie Manifold, Dave Lucas, Elizabeth Harvey, Chris Bosley, Luke Theochari, Howard Cheese, Keith Seume, Peter Stevens, Ilse Bohn and Shaun Hollamby.

Except where indicated otherwise, all photographs were taken by the author using a Pentax K1000 camera and Fuji 35 mm film.

Front Cover
The fastest 'vintage' Beetle in the world, Keith Seume's turbo car is capable of turning the quarter mile in less than 10 secs.

Back Cover (*top*)
Star of ITV's soap opera 'Emmerdale', Glenda McKay takes the famous number 53 to 'full bore' at Brands Hatch.

(*bottom*)
Dr David Enderby's Cosworth powered Ghia approaching 160 mph in a round of the British Thundersaloons Championships.

Contents

Introduction

The Volkswagen Beetle is without doubt an automotive work of genius, an enigma, a phenomenon whose quite remarkable production life, which now spans more than half a century, shows every sign of being continued well into the future. Down through the years, Beetles have been used for every conceivable purpose on land and water and the evergreen air-cooled flat-four engine has even successfully powered many thousands of light aircraft but, contrary to popular belief, it is in the heady and exciting world of motor sport that the Beetle has scored some of its most illustrious successes.

The car's role in competition started during the 1950s and although in standard form doesn't, at first glance, appear to possess any of the credentials required for success in out-and-out speed events, the humble, tail-happy Volkswagen has been to the fore in both national and international competition for more than 40 years.

In the early days after the war when production of the People's car was at last under way, the Porsche-designed VW was equipped with a diminutive 1131cc

Quite so . . .

1

One of the twentieth century's finest and most innovative engineers, Dr Ferdinand Porsche, designer of the Beetle and the Auto-Union Grand Prix car.

engine developing an equally unimpressive 25 bhp and a chassis whose narrow track, swing-axle rear suspension offered bags of oversteer almost at a moment's notice, a facet which quickly earned the Beetle an unjust and inaccurate reputation for unsatisfactory roadholding.

However, the basic design, originally laid down by Porsche's studios in 1931 was correct, albeit in need of development. Not that Dr Porsche had ever envisaged that his passenger saloon would take to the race track. As is recorded in great detail elsewhere, the Beetle was made for the specific purpose of carrying a family of four on German autobahns at a maximum cruising speed of around 70 mph all day and every day for many years at which it acquitted itself extremely well.

Because the development of the Beetle during the 1930s ran roughly parallel to that of the Auto-Union Grand Prix car, also designed by Porsche, it was inevitable that both cars were to share many of the same engineering design principles unlikely as it may seem.

Torsion-bar suspension (patented by Porsche in 1931), a rear-mounted engine and a gearbox/transaxle unit were all very dear to the good doctor's heart and although highly unconventional at the time, the theory, when put into practice worked especially well.

The German ace driver, Bernd Rosemeyer who, prior to 1935 had never handled anything more powerful than a 45 bhp DKW motorcycle used the V16 Auto-Union P-Wagen to terrible effect against the more powerful Grand Prix cars from Daimler-Benz throughout 1935 and 1936. In his second Grand Prix ever,

A restored C-Type Auto-Union, the true forerunner of today's Formula One cars and whose development ran parallel to that of the VW Beetle. (Photo: Audi Press)

Rosemeyer was just pipped to the post by the vastly experienced Rudolf Caracciola (Mercedes-Benz) winning his first Grand Prix just a few months later.

Mounted 'on' his Auto-Union, Rosemeyer won the 1936 European Championship outright in addition to two mountain hill climbs and two non-championship Grand Prix. Not that everyone who drove for the Auto-Union team achieved the success of the young and dashing Rosemeyer. The rear weight bias of the P-Wagen allied to formidable power (375 bhp from five litres) was something completely new in Grand Prix racing at this time but, Rosemeyer, having graduated straight from motorcycles knew no differently and quickly mastered what was generally thought to be an ill-handling motor car.

For devotees of the Beetle, the above is an all-too-familiar story. The many millions of converts who understand the joys of 'opposite lock' motoring and who have learned the skills necessary to derive the most from their Volkswagens remain unconvinced to this day by the critics who continue droning from their armchairs about the Beetle's unsuitability for competition despite overwhelming evidence to the contrary.

Unlike more conventional motor cars, tuning a Volkswagen for both power and reliability at the same time has never been particularly easy nor for that matter cheap. The limits imposed by air cooling particularly before the days of specialist Volkswagen tuning companies were considerable, would-be rally champions relying on the car's inherent ruggedness and strength to gain high placings in national and international events.

However, despite all the seemingly apparent drawbacks of a car that has a reputation for being slow, noisy and a complete inability to go round corners quickly and safely, people from all over the world have successfully competed in a variety of events with Beetles often displacing much more powerful cars into the bargain.

In every branch of motor sport during the past four decades, Beetle drivers have rarely been far away from the winner's rostrum; rallying, circuit racing, trialing, autocross, drag racing, long-distance offroading and autotesting — name it and the Beetle has done it. An underdog which has won through against all odds, it is obvious from the car's track record that the Beetle has considerably more to offer than its standard specification would suggest.

Over engineered to the point where, on even the world's roughest and toughest rally routes on which, many conventional cars have been quite literally shaken to pieces, the Beetle would hold together to fight another day.

So strong is its body, chassis, gearbox and engine that, for many competition purposes, the Beetle requires little in the way of strengthening. Of course if you want to and you are rich enough, you can spend thousands of pounds preparing a car for whatever branch of sport you prefer but one of the great beauties of the Beetle is that there are also events for impecunious youngsters who can satisfy their curiosity and need to experience the full bite of competitiveness without going to the considerable trouble and expense of building a pukka racer.

Drag racing is just one example of a sport where anyone who holds an ordinary driving licence and a roadworthy Beetle can turn up at Santa Pod for example and

The German ace driver, Bernd Rosemeyer showed time and again that the correct place for the engine is behind the driver and not in front of him.

Neil Corner's beautifully restored Auto-Union was given an airing at the 1991 Christie's Festival, Silverstone.

JLT 420, the famous two-tone blue 1947 Beetle belonging to Peter Colborne-Baber whose father John, a Surrey-based motor dealer was responsible for putting Beetles on the map in Britain.

Major Ivan Hirst of the Royal Electrical and Mechanical Engineers who was in charge of the Volkswagen factory after the War and without whom, the Beetle may not have been as successful as it is.

have a lot of fun in the 'Run what you brung' class. You may not win a trophy and you most definitely will not record the fastest time of the day but to the real Beetle enthusiast, taking part in a colourful and worthwhile spectacle of motoring fun is more important than winning.

If on the other hand, you are more interested in driving special stages and experiencing the joys of sideways, as opposed to straight-line motoring, today's thriving historic rally scene may be what you're looking for. Both drag racing and historic rallying have grown up from virtually nothing during the past 10 years in Britain and the rest of Europe and provide the amateur with a challenge which in most circumstances won't break the bank.

Beetles thrive on rallies and the rougher the better. The well-known veteran rally driver Bob Beales (and more of him later) has already shown that a combination of his considerable driving talent and a well-prepared Beetle can still beat the best of the rest in the 1990s and what better motive can one have for entering an historic rally than wanting to beat the all-conquering Lotus Cortinas and Mini Coopers?

Rallying in the rough not your scene? Well, thanks to 'Olly' Hollamby and his son Shaun, both long-time Beetle campaigners, we in Britain now have a fully-fledged Beetle racing championship. Almost into its third year, this British racing championship has not only proved very successful for competitors and spectators but has also attracted a great deal of media attention, not to mention a number of media personalities who like Chris Goffey, star of the BBC's motoring programme 'Top Gear', have taken up the challenge of this demanding sport with great enthusiasm.

And if rallying, drag racing and circuit racing don't appeal to you, there is always 'mud-plugging' at which the Beetle excels, autocross, rallycross, night rallies and club treasure hunts to name but a few.

Of the people who have driven Beetles in competition down through the years, the vast majority still speak fondly of their memories and of the Beetles that allowed them to take part. For the purpose of writing this book, I have interviewed a good many people who, although in many instances have long since retired from active motor sport, continue to get excited about the prospect of driving Beetles.

Some haven't driven a Beetle for years but others have wisely kept their old competition cars, carefully stored in garages and some occasionally get used for the purpose they were originally intended. During the course of this book, I have not only tried to convey my own enthusiasm for Beetles but the enthusiasm of those people who have and continue to have a passion for what many regard as the world's greatest motor car.

If you, dear reader, are new to Beetles or if you most definitely are not, if you have taken part in competition or would like to, the intention of this humble tome is simply to add fuel to the spark that encouraged you to buy it in the first place. If you are not convinced that Beetles have a healthy place in the world of motoring competition, you need read no further but . . . I hope you do.

CHAPTER ONE

Rallying to the cause

To the enlightened few, the introduction of the Volkswagen Beetle to the world's markets in the late 1940s and early 1950s was a breath of fresh air. The highly individual nature of the car's unusual specification and styling endeared itself to those for whom the mundane nature of the majority of conventional cars was not good enough. Post-War 'grey porridge' especially from Britain was far from exciting, not especially reliable and to a great extent, well past its sell-by date.

Here in Britain, devotees of the Beetle will be for ever grateful to John Colborne-Baber, a Surrey car dealer who saw one of these funny German cars for the first time in 1947. Colborne in fact took a Beetle in part-exchange for a car he sold to a Swedish chap travelling in this country and immediately became hooked.

After the War, many ex-servicemen returning home naturally arrived in Beetles. John Colborne-Baber snapped up as many as he could and offered them for sale with the choice of leather seats, bright gloss paintwork (remember, the cars arriving from the factory until 1949 all had matt paintwork) and a right-hand-drive conversion.

With their skinny 16-inch cross-ply tyres, cable brakes, 'crash' gearbox, narrow track and limited visibility through the split rear window, Beetles appeared to offer little to the sporting enthusiast especially when you consider that the diminutive flat-four engine developed no more than 25 bhp.

A few year ago, the late John Colborne-Baber's son, Peter very kindly allowed me to drive JLT 420, the sole surviving 1947 Beetle bought by his father from an ex-serviceman shortly after the War and, having spent nearly a week enjoying this historic relic, I was able to satisfy myself as to why so many people were and still are so enthusiastic about Beetles, old and new.

Resplendent in its famous two-tone blue paintwork, old JLT, which is still a left-hooker having never been converted to right-hand drive, was absolutely delightful in every respect despite having covered some 300,000 miles since new.

It started on the button first time every time, revved cleanly, sounded strong and sat happily on the M4 at between 60-70 mph without once ever complaining. Alright the cable brakes were something of a liability in modern traffic, the semaphore indicators weren't immediately apparent to other road users and the six-volt lighting system was absolutely shocking but otherwise brought a big beaming smile to my face and to the faces of people who, for one reason and another, hadn't seen such an old Beetle being driven on the road for a good many years.

One of the earliest appearances of a Beetle in competition was on the Monte-Carlo Rally. This drawing shows Nathan and Schellhaas on the 1952 event. (Picture: Castrol Achievements)

International star of the 1950s and '60s, Bill Bengry won the 1960 RAC Championship in WVJ 606, a Tomato Red 1200 which he still has to this day.

One of the sport's greatest characters, Bill Bengry finds time for a cultural interlude in Stuttgart prior to the start of one of the many international rallies in which he competed in Beetles.

To prove that Bengry's 1960 RAC Championship win was no fluke, he repeated the victory in 1961. Here, he is seen with his long-time navigator, David Skeffington at a time control on the 1961 RAC.

This wasn't quite the 'ultimate driving experience' but, for me, it came close and demonstrated perfectly what old man Porsche was getting at when he laid the foundations for his People's car more than a decade previously.

JLT 420 was never used for serious competition work but serves to illustrate, along with other Beetles from the same period that the nature of the beast had great potential.

Now although Beetles were never used in any great numbers until well into the 1950s for competition purposes, there were three very special alloy-bodied cars built by Porsche before the outbreak of World War Two that were based on Volkswagen components and intended to take part in the 1939 Berlin to Rome race.

The cars were beautifully streamlined coupes built on a standard Beetle chassis but fitted with a tuned and 'bored out' 1.5-litre engine. The cars had a top speed of around 90 mph but thanks to Adolf Hitler's absurd antics and insane ambition to take over the world, the 1939 race from Berlin to Rome never took place.

In addition to the Beetle project, Dr Porsche and his son, Ferry had harboured a long-held ambition to create their own sporting cars and the streamlined coupe, Type 60K10 marks their first attempt to do so. Many consider the car to be the true forerunner of the 356 Porsche which, for many years after the first prototype was sold in July 1948, kept closely to its roots in utilizing Volkswagen components.

It is interesting that in his excellent autobiography 'Cars are my life' (published by Patrick Stephens Ltd), Ferry Porsche writes, "Despite the demands of the VW programme, we had of course never abandoned our own racing plans. Indeed, the VW provided an almost perfect basis for further developments in this direction."

The 'streamliner' as a design study was a great success although it didn't see active service on the race track but, as Ferry Porsche adds, "In terms of handling and performance represented a considerable step forward."

Incidentally, Dr Porsche used one of these cars for his own personal enjoyment for a while but, alas, only one of the trio is still in existence today.

From the above, it is possible to draw the conclusion that if the Beetle was a satisfactory basis on which to go racing for a truly great and brilliant engineer like Ferry Porsche, it is certainly good enough for the rest of us.

Naturally, a number of critics have sought to discredit the principle of air-cooling over the years despite overwhelming evidence not only that it works but also that it works exceptionally well . . . too well for comfort on occasions too.

Porsche's record at Le Mans and at all the other great sports car races over the years with virtually all their cars from the original 356 through the 917 to the 962 shows perfectly that developing a sound idea to its ultimate conclusion is often better than chopping and changing in the hope that the trial and error theory will eventually lead to success.

And the same theory was applied by the people at Wolfsburg who, between 1945 and 1978 incorporated more than 70,000 modifications into the Beetle in an attempt to perfect what was basically sound in the first place.

Porsche of course went their own way after the War and the Volkswagen factory, rejuvenated in 1945 by the British occupation force concentrated on making non-sporting Saloons. The Beetle was after all intended as transport for two adults and their children and not for pounding around rally courses and racing circuits.

In the early days, there was another snag for sporting motorists who felt the urge to compete. There were no events in which they could take part. The outbreak of War had cancelled the Berlin-Rome race in September 1939 and after the War, the last thing on most people's minds was the organisation of motoring events.

A number of competitive events were run both here in Britain and abroad towards the end of the 1940s but most were local low-key affairs with some exceptions and rallying, as we think of it today, was still in its infancy.

The types of competition for which Beetles and other saloons were eligible in the early 1950s were more in the nature of driving tests with the exception of the Monte Carlo Rally which had survived from pre-war days. Beetles certainly made the odd appearance in the Monte but never achieved high placings at the finish.

Engine power was limited and tuning equipment virtually non-existent. A rally-prepared Beetle was about the same as a cooking shopping Beetle except for a couple of spotlights mounted on the front bumper and another one on the roof if its owner's bank account could stretch that far.

However, what is significant about those events of 40 years ago, few that there were, is that the often impecunious people who took part in them, may not have been able to drive very quickly but they sure had one hell of a lot more fun than the highly-paid professionals who drive highly-complex works cars in similar events today.

The last time Bengry's famous Beetle was used in anger was on the RAC's Golden Fifty Rally in 1982, an event which scattered the seeds for today's thriving historic rally movement.

Knowing Bill, he probably forgot to bank the cheque . . .

It was obvious from 1951 that the Irish would take to the Beetle more quickly
than any other nation in Europe including the Germans. Stephen O'Flaherty began
his business officially importing Beetles and also owned a Dublin-based factory
assembling Beetles from CKD kits two years before the first imports started
trickling into Britain.

The Beetle was relatively cheap to buy and economical to run but it was also
strong and tough and well able to stand the rigours of a thrash along Irish roads.

14

WVJ 606 today awaiting a full restoration.

Beetles were especially successful on the East African Safari Rally. This is Barbour and Doughty on their way to 7th place in 1966. (Photo: East African Safari Illustrated)

At the finish of the '66 Safari, Barbour and Doughty received a cash award from the Safari Committee and a prize from Bosch. (Photo: East African Safari Illustrated)

Mike Hinde was an early convert to the Beetle fold. Here he is seen in Dr Robert Ball's 1200 winning the 1958 Welsh Rally. (Photo: Wrekin Photo Services)

Beetles were successful in hillclimb events until the Mini Coopers came along. Note the driver's 'pudding-basin' crash helnet. (Photo: James Brymer)

Mike Hinde winning the saloon car class at the Rhydymwyn Sprint meeting. The car is fitted with a roll-top sunroof but no rollcage which would not be allowed today. (Photo: Photographic Craftsmen Ltd)

Anyone who has driven any distance in Ireland, north or south, will know just how rough the going can get at times but the Beetle was able to take any amount of abuse that was thrown at it.

As time went on, more and more people took to the Beetle including the legendary Paddy Hopkirk who of course went on to considerable success in the 1960s with Mini Coopers.

Contemporary reports in the sporting journals often cite the early Irish competitions as some of the most exciting jaunts of their day. The majority included out-and-out tests of driving skill, often held on public roads, the drivers pitting their wits against strategically placed cones.

The great names of the day, apart from Hopkirk, included Kevin Sherry who won the 1959 Circuit of Ireland in a Beetle, T. P. O'Connell, Declan O'Leary and Arthur Ryan to name but a few and their skill behind the wheel of a Beetle is still talked about in Ireland to this day.

The Irish and Beetles actually make for a great partnership. Both are loveable and both have a degree of charismatic eccentricity which is hard to resist. It was with this is mind that I ventured across the Irish Sea in the Autumn of 1991 for a re-run of the Circuit of Ireland, an exciting three-day event exclusively for historic cars.

Amongst the usual turn-out of Minis, Cortinas, MGs, Aston Martins and a number of other delectable machines, there were of course a number of Beetles

Mike Hinde with just some of the trophies he won in Beetles. (Photo: Mike Hinde)

taking part and when there are several Irishmen taking part in the 'Circuit' in Beetles, you just have to be there to savour the action.

Brian Kahoe had entered his 1300, Reggie McSpadden brought along his fairly standard and recently restored 1500 and that great character, Paddy O'Callaghan who incidentally, was rarely without his pipe in his mouth was also embedded firmly behind the wheel of his 1302S one of 12 Beetles owned by the ex-Volkswagen dealer.

In addition, there was the great Ronnie Adams (who won the very first Circuit of Ireland in 1936) driving a Beetle for the first time in his life, George McMillan driving a very special Beetle-based replica of the 1959 718 RSK Porsche Spyder and arguably two of the most talented Beetle drivers of all time in the form of Robert Woodside and Bob Beales. Bob is the only Englishman in the pack but had taken his 1958 Beetle across the water to Belfast for the start in a friendly attempt to beat the Irish boys at their own game.

A major rally held over 500 miles of Ireland's very best rally territory, the cars headed from Belfast in a south-westerly direction towards Morraghan taking in a few driving tests on the way. Driving tests are always a good way of breaking into a proper rally and the displays of skill exhibited particularly by McMillan (a past autotest champion), Woodside, Beales and O'Callaghan had to be witnessed to be believed.

The whole idea of an autotest is simple. You have a small area of tarmac' and a tight course, marked out by cones which has to be negotiated as quickly as possible. Handbrake turns, opposite lock and maximum revs are the order of the day with a few massive broadside sweeps thrown in for good measure.

With his larger-than-life character and great bulk, O'Callaghan was impressive to say the least throwing the 1302S around with complete abandon and Woodside's performances were simply breathtaking but it was Beales who came out on top on this occasion, the little 1300cc twin-carb 75 bhp Okrasa engine crying for all it was worth.

Anyone who has seen Bob Beales in action or had the pleasure (and pain) of sitting in the passenger seat of his famous yellow and black car, will know that he never does anything by halves and although his style is never anything less than spectacular and on the 'ragged edge', he is always able to put in an incomprehensibly fast time.

His Beetle, an ex-Bill Bengry car which Bob laughingly boasts has been around the clock three times and on its roof twice, is also sufficient testimony to the inherent strength of the Beetle. Contrary to popular belief, it is not highly modified either but its performance does demonstrate admirably that a carefully assembled engine (performed by tuning wizard, Tim Kemp) and a well-prepared vehicle can pay dividends even though the power output is not that great. Again, it's the chap in the driving seat that counts most in rally circles.

And after the initial series of special tests, it was Beales who emerged the fastest of the Beetle drivers with Woodside running a close second. Throughout the night, they fought hard on the long road sections, the wonderful and distinctive

Bob Beales searches for his engine . . .

Ah . . . there it is.

cacophony of the flat-fours being audible well above the familiar growl of the more conventional machinery.

Punctures, which have always played a prominent role in deciding the final outcome of a rally, delayed both Reggie McSpadden who was putting up an admirable performance in his 1500 and George McMillan who, in his open-top car was suffering badly from fatigue and tiredness.

After a brief rest at Sligo, the circus concentrated its efforts for the remainder of the competition on a number of special tests and regularity runs aimed at stretching navigational skills around the picturesque countryside surrounding Galway on the west coast of this enchanting island.

This was Irish rallying at its best and although, after three gruelling days, the crews were fairly exhausted from their efforts, they had all succeeded in recreating the truly golden days of the sport. True to form, none of the Beetles suffered any mechanical maladies with the exception of dear old Paddy O'Callaghan who reported that his twin Dellorto carburettors had developed 'flat spots'. Incidentally, Paddy won the Circuit of Ireland outright in 1966 but on this occasion, had to settle for eighth position.

Bob Beales was the highest finisher of the Beetle drivers in sixth place with Reggie McSpadden right behind him in seventh. King of the autotesters, Robert Woodside was ninth, Brian Kahoe finished a creditable 24th and George McMillan was content with 28th. Ronnie Adams was well down in 54th after a couple of navigational errors upset any ideas of a top-ten finish but Ronnie, at 75 years of age was still able to show a clean pair of heels to the 50 or so competitors who came in behind him.

A truly remarkable performance from everyone but why were these underpowered little cars able to beat so many of the high-performance exotica, including a couple of Porsche 911s and the same number of Aston Martins?

Bob Beales may have hit the nail on the head when he said after the event, "One of the reasons why we were so successful is that sometimes it is an advantage not to have too much power. You have to concentrate harder in a Beetle and if you get every corner right, you can gain several seconds or even minutes over a long road section. Someone with a Lotus Cortina which develops in excess of 110 bhp can always make up for mistakes on the bends by booting it hard down the straight. With a Beetle, you can boot it as hard as you like on a straight but you will never make up for time lost in the corners."

And Beales should know because he won the Welsh Historic Rally Championship outright in 1992 driving his trusty and much used '58. Incidentally, Beales's Beetle which he has owned since 1965, originally saw service as a 24-hours-a-day taxi.

But if the Irish put the Beetle on the competition map in national events like the Circuit of Ireland, it was in the East African Safari Rally that Beetles came to the fore on the international stage. Arguably the most demanding rally in the world (with the exception of the recent Paris Dakar raids), the Safari was first run in 1953.

A real marathon designed to test cars and crews to the limit, in which it

Driving a Beetle quickly demands accuracy and skill in the corners. Firstly, you have to set the car off balance . . .

. . . then, flick out the tail

and power away, if you can see through the dust. (Photos: Bob Beales)

Paddy O'Callaghan (outright winner of the 1966 Circuit of Ireland) negotiates a bend in a modern 'historic' event.

Reggie McSpadden and Paddy O'Callaghan, two of the all-time great Irish drivers . . .

. . . not forgetting Robert Woodside.

An additional oil cooler at the front of the car can help enormously in rallying provided that the pipes are kept well out of harm's way.

succeeded and continues to succeed in doing to this day, the 2,000 mile course was run across some of the world's most inhospitable but beautiful countryside. It was rough, the roads were often non-existent and sudden thunderstorms frequently threatened the roads that did exist.

Add all that to the dangers imposed by dust and sand storms, not to mention large, wild animals straying across your path and you've got one powerful test of endurance.

Needless to say, the VW was an ideal candidate for such a rally in the 1950s where the superior traction offered by the rear-mounted engine and gearbox paid handsome dividends. And, as if to endorse the point, Alan Dix drove his 1200 to victory on that very first event. His win was no fluke either because a Beetle won again the following year, in 1957 and 1962. Beetles also scored class wins in 1955, 1960, 1964 and 1965 and team prizes in 1953, 1954, 1955, 1957 and 1958 an impressive record which speaks for itself.

It is not the intention of this author to give a blow-by-blow account of the excitement of each event for fear of boring you, dear reader, into a deep sleep but over the many years in which Beetles took part in the Safari, there were some inevitable low points to accompany the high points.

The 'vintage' Safari year was 1957 when Beetles filled the top three places driven by Gus Holmann, P. Townsend and Jim Cardwell respectively but move on a few

A bite to eat before the start of a long event is always a good idea provided you're not the kind of navigator who suffers from travel sickness.

Maestro at work, Robert Woodside is virtually unbeatable at the art of autotesting.

Ronnie Adams won the very first Circuit of Ireland way back in 1936 but, proving that it's never too late to start Beetling, he is competing here at the wheel of a 1600 for the first time at the age of 75.

George McMillan drives an open-top GP Spyder in modern events. His car is a Beetle-based replica of the 1959 718 RSK Porsche.

27

One of the most talented 'new boys', Irishman George McMillan is a past national autotest champion.

A true gentleman and a fine driver, Brian Kahoe rarely misses an opportunity to have some fun in a Beetle.

years to the mid-1960s and it is obvious from the results that the Beetle, despite considerable development, was at last being outclassed by increasingly sophisticated cars from Ford, Peugeot, Rover, Volvo, Merecedes-Benz and the rest.

Take 1966 for example. By this time, Volkswagen had introduced the 1300 model and although, in standard form its power output at 40 bhp was a great improvement over the 34 bhp 1200, it still lagged some way behind its rivals. Take one 1300 engine and tune it to give 70 bhp and it was good but not quite good enough to ensure victory.

Having said that, a performance deficit didn't prevent Richard Barbour and Mike Doughty taking their 1300 to seventh place in 1966 with a magnificent effort that captured the imagination of many thousands of Beetle enthusiasts who lined the route that year.

On this occasion, Barbour and Doughty used a standard car purchased new from the showroom of Northern Motors in Kitale. The Beetle was relieved of its rear seats which were substituted more usefully for spare wheels and tyres, additional lights were fitted up front, the cylinder heads were polished and the standard crossply road tyres were exchanged for 'mud-grip' rubber.

From the start at Nairobi, the car ran almost faultlessly. Over a very wet stretch between Korogwe and Dar-es-Salaam, the starter motor gave a little trouble but then the car was being asked to act as a motor boat on occasions. "The VW fully

Servicing the RSK Porsche replica is a good deal easier than servicing a Beetle saloon.

Not a lot of room in the cockpit of the RSK, a car that was never designed for the rough and tumble of rallying.

Reggie McSpadden demonstrates that you can have just as much fun and be just as successful in a completely standard Beetle.

met our expectations'' said Barbour. "The Beetle cornered beautifully and hugged the narrow slippery roads. We were only held up for a couple of minutes by cars stuck in front of us and we negotiated the mountains without incident . . . we had no trouble at all on the dash across the Rift Valley and as we approached Kampala, we were lying second overall and getting increasingly confident.'' By the finish at Nairobi, the car had dropped to seventh thanks to an altercation with a rock which broke a track rod but the performance of Barbour and Doughty demonstrated that the Beetle might have been a little down but it certainly wasn't out.

By stark contrast, 1967 was a disastrous year for Beetles. Of the twelve that started, just five finished and the highest placed of those was in 19th position once again driven by Barbour and Doughty.

Apart from the tremendous pace set by the Fords and Peugeots, the Beetle's main enemy this year was dust which got into everything including the engines of some cars. The highly-tuned Okrasa engines recommended by Scania-Vabis, the Swedish Volkswagen importers, worked splendidly on the roads around the Arctic Circle but just weren't right for the very different conditions encountered in Africa.

Bill Bengry retired with a cracked sump, Tommy Fjastad overall winner in 1962 crashed, his car subsequently setting fire to itself and Khan and Neuter dropped out after one too many punctures tried their patience too far. In all, it was a disastrous year for Beetles and the last in which a significant team effort was made in any numbers.

Throughout the 1950s and '60s, Beetles made appearances in hundreds of different rallies not only in Africa, Eire, Britain and Europe but in Australia as well. The car was so admirably suited to particularly rough conditions that almost anyone who could drive a Beetle properly was almost assured of some kind of prize at the end of an event.

One In A Million

No chapter on rallying would be complete without recourse to the driving career of Bill Bengry, an English garage proprietor who, as far is Britain is concerned, did more to hit home the Beetle message than just about anyone else.

A colourful and complicated character blessed with quick wit and keen intelligence, Bill was amongst the first British Volkswagen dealers and quickly came to appreciate the car's qualities. From the mid-1950s onwards, he was amazingly successful driving a number of different cars including works' Rovers and Peugeots and even a Rolls-Royce Silver Shadow on the 1970 London to Mexico Rally but it is the Beetle for which he holds the most affection today.

His first national success came in 1956 in the Mobilgas Economy Run when he scored a class win having managed to wring an average of 43 mpg from his 1200 Beetle MCJ 191. Admittedly, economy runs may not be considered 'proper' rallies in most quarters but the competitive element was extremely strong all the same.

Bengry entered the same car (which was sadly broken up a few years ago) for a

A triumverate of talent. Robert Woodside, Reggie McSpadden and Paddy O'Callaghan await their turn patiently to start a driving test on the 1991 Circuit of Ireland retrospective historic rally.

Beetles remain competitive today in historic rallies even when pitted against Cortinas, Saabs, Healeys and Mini Coopers.

Dave Lucas competed in a variety of national and international events during the 1970s in his 1302S.

By the mid-1970s, Beetles were outclassed on events like the RAC but a lack of power never prevented Dave Lucas having a go. He is seen here in his trusty 1302S on the 1974 RAC International. (Photo: Foster and Skeffington)

Dave Lucas was successful at rallying, circuit racing and classic reliability trials and went on to organise the now-defunct Birmingham Superprix. Here, he is seen with the well-known works Porsche driver, Derek Bell.

Francis Tuthill has a large collection of Beetles including a number of rally-prepared machines with which he continues to be successful.

number of different rallies over the next three years beating more powerful machinery time and again including a Porsche 356 on one of the tough Welsh events in 1957 but it was with WVJ 606, a 1960 Tomato Red 1200 and XVJ 230 that he scored his most resounding success.

By the end of the 1950s, the Beetle with little more than 34 bhp on offer was beginning to be hopelessly outclassed by the opposition. It simply didn't have the 'grunt' to keep up with the opposition let alone beat it but Bengry, ever-determined to prove the sceptics wrong, took WVJ 606 to outright victory in the 1960 RAC Championship.

And to prove that his title was not just good luck, he did exactly the same thing the following year, retaining his title into the bargain. Perhaps more interestingly, he scored both championship wins in virtually standard Beetles. After all, Bill had a business to run and didn't have the time (and still hasn't to this day at over 70 years of age) to start tuning and 'tweaking' his car.

Rally preparation then included removing the hub caps, fitting additional spotlights and removing the front anti-roll bar. The latter was a factory modification introduced in 1960 aimed at reducing oversteer but Bill liked oversteer in abundant quantities and exploited its advantages to great effect at every opportunity.

Engine modifications were limited to polishing and porting the cylinder heads and altering the venturi in the carburettor but Bengry's demon tweak for the 1960 season was little more than the fitment of the then newly introduced Pirelli Cintura tyres. The early ones gave problems, Bengry suffering endless punctures on the RAC International of that same year.

However, the manufacturers were quick to identify the cause of the problem and re-launched the improved version as a Cinturato. Anyone who has driven a Beetle on crossplies will fully understand what a marvellous handling aid radials are and Bengry was quick, in both senses, in exploiting them.

On one occasion during the 1960 Championship season, Bengry and his long-time navigator David Skeffington got into deep trouble from which there was no escape even with radial tyres. On the famous road section between Abergwesyn and Tregaron in mid-Wales, a river which at one point of the course normally runs under a road bridge, had broken its banks with dire consequences for the rally.

The majority of competitors found an alternative route but Bengry put his faith in the fact that Beetles are water-tight and duly attempted to cross the river. It was a mistake. The car was swept for several hundred yards downstream, our intrepid heroes being quickly engulfed in muddy water to chest height.

Such was the external water pressure that opening the doors became a real struggle but when the car eventually came to a halt, Bill and David managed to grab hold of the spotlight on the roof and pull themselves to safety. "We were both very cold and soaked through to the skin" says Bill, "and decided to take off our trousers and underwear. As you can imagine, we both looked bloody ridiculous because we had to return home to our wives with our jumpers stretched around our knees."

Despite that hiccup, Bengry's success in Beetles led to several jaunts on the East

With a specially built 2.4-litre engine and 174 bhp, Francis Tuthill became the terror of the Ford Escort brigade in the 1980s. (Photo: Francis Tuthill)

Some years ago, Francis Tuthill built a private museum in the grounds of his house in which to keep his cars. The roof is appropriately decorated.

Tuthill competed in the 1977 London-to-Sydney Marathon in his 'Rainbow' Beetle, a car which has raised a great deal of money for charity. (Photo: Banbury Guardian)

Mike Hinde and Dennis Greenslade have combined their considerable talents to tackle the world of historic rallying in Mike's Okrasa-engined 1957 Beetle. Here, the car is in a marvellous drift on its way to a most creditable sixth place and first in class on the 1993 Kerridge Rally. (Photo: Speedsports)

African Safari but for the 1967 event, he was one of the VW drivers whose 1500 engine was wrecked by heat distortion and sand finding its way into the bores.

The Safari Beetles were all prepared by the Cooper Motor Corporation of Nairobi and not by the crews of each car which meant that Bengry could safely retain his own 1960 car for events in this country.

For several years after retiring from rallying in the mid-1970s, he used his RAC Championship winner as an everyday road car but when, in 1982, the RAC announced that it would be celebrating its 50th anniversary with a special historic rally, Bill spent some time rebuilding the car and treated it to a new coat of paint. At the time of writing, that same car is in the process of undergoing its first proper restoration after which, Bill intends to use it once again in historic events.

Incidentally, when the Volkswagen Type 3 was announced in 1961, Bengry was one of the first people in the world to use one for rallying when not competing in his Beetle and, inspired by his win in a round of the 1962 Motoring News Championship, a number of other well known rally stars became Volkswagen mounted including Reggie McSpadden and Robert McBurney from Ireland.

No 'Works' Team

Although by this time, there were many long-distance events held on the European continent, the major manufacturers and private teams alike considered the RAC International to be the most prestigious, success in which was the most likely to bump up sales in the showroom. Unfortunately, Volkswagen never took the opportunity to enter an official 'works' team in any type of event with Beetles but, in 1963, the Swedish Volkswagen importers, Scania Vabis scored second place overall in the RAC with a 1500S driven by Harry Kallstrom and, encouraged by their surprise success, returned to Britain the following year with a team of Beetles powered by special 1300 Okrasa engines.

The factory at Wolfsburg, whilst the Beetle was in production, never encouraged speed tuning modifications of any kind. A sporting Volkswagen didn't fit in with the marketing image of an 'alternative' family saloon built for reliability and longevity.

If you wanted to drive quickly, the Beetle was the wrong car for you so, why not go and buy a Porsche instead? A reasonable view certainly but, not everyone could afford a Porsche and not everyone who could afford one actually wanted one, preferring to stick with their trusty Beetles instead.

Devotion by so many to the little car resulted in the rapid expansion of specialist tuning companies like Okrasa in Germany and Speedwell in Britain (of which the Grand Prix driver Graham Hill was a director) who capitalised on what was a rapidly growing market of Beetle people with Porsche aspirations.

For Volkswagen owners who had cash to spare during the 1950s and '60s, Okrasa would duly oblige those who were less than content with their 25, 30 or 34 bhp standard Beetles by offering complete engine tuning kits capable of boosting power to a competitive level.

Historic rallying is every bit as demanding as the original rallies which the Historic Rally Car Register seeks to emulate. Beetles, being able to float, are able to tackle fords like this better than most cars. (Photo: Speedsports)

Fitting a supercharger used to be a popular, if slightly expensive means of extracting more power from the flat-four but, thanks to the Americans, they are now no longer necessary.

Monte Carlo Challenge 1990

Arguably, the world's best Beetle driver, Bob Beales has been winning rallies in his famous yellow and black Beetle for a quarter of a century and is the 1992 Welsh Champion.

A three-man crew prepares for the start of the 1990 Monte-Carlo Historic Rally. From left to right, Ron Beales, Colin Ellis and Bob Beales.

The kits consisted of larger barrels and pistons 'bored out' to 1295cc, a heavy-duty long-stroke crankshaft with 69.5 mm stroke and special twin-port cylinder heads to improve breathing. The compression ratio was increased to 7.5:1 and two Solex 32 PICB carburettors replaced the constricting single Solex item fitted to the standard engines.

With the ability to rev cleanly above 6,000 rpm, a Beetle fitted with an Okrasa unit was capable of 100 mph-plus performance and, as Berndt Jansson's eighth position overall in the 1963 RAC Rally shows, was more than able to 'mix it' with the big boys who, at the time, considered anything less than a Healey 3000, Mini Cooper or Lotus Cortina to be an 'also ran'.

The seeds sewn by Bill Bengry and the Scania Vabis team particularly during the 1960s gave inspiration to the many who followed. It is true to say that much of the success of the Beetle in both national and international competition up to the mid-1960s had been dependent on adverse weather conditions which brought the speed of the herd down to that of those struggling with the limited output of the flat-four.

When the V4 Saab 96 and all-conquering Ford Escort twin-cams came along in 1968, few drivers in anything else would get a look in on the winner's rostrum but the glorious rally days of the Beetle were far from over. Volkswagen-Porsche of Austria entered a team of Beetles for the 1972 Austrian Alpine Rally against the factory works teams from Lancia, Fiat, Saab and BMW.

Driven by G. Janger and H. Gottlieb, one 1302S finished a most impressive second overall in the general classification behind the winning Fiat 124 Spider whereas the similar car of Grunsteldl and Hopf came in fourth just behind a Saab V4 but in front of the Porsche 911S of Haberl and Fritz.

A report on the rally which appeared in the October 1972 issue of 'Motor Sport' magazine pointed out that "Some of the stages were inclined to be rough, though it was noticeable that the complainants were mainly those with not-so-rugged cars at their disposal." In other words, here was yet another glowing testimony to the inherent strength of the Beetle and its ability to withstand the horrors of some of Europe's roughest roads.

During the 1973 international season, the very best cars from Ford, Saab, Lancia and the rest would ignore the threat from the Austrian Volkswagen-Porsche entry at their peril as the Beetles were always willing and able to get in amongst them at a moment's notice.

However, apart from the efforts of the Austrian team, the Beetle's role in top level rally sport during the 1970s was very much diminished. A few courageous privateers carried on in the hope of gaining a class win but the days when an enthusiastic amateur could jump aboard a stock saloon and keep pace with the leaders were well and truly over.

Any event in which a Beetle was entered by this time would attract large crowds of Volkswagen enthusiasts, naturally, but they were there cheering on their heroes in desperate hope rather than with a realistic sense of victory. Even so, it was always good to see a Beetle being used in competition.

Throughout the 1970s, the Birmingham solicitor Dave Lucas flew the Wolfsburg

Bob Beales demonstrates the art of Beetle driving in a full opposite-lock slide practising for the 1990 Longleat Stages Rally. (Photo: David Burdon-Bailey)

Things don't always go to plan. Five miles into the 1990 Longleat event, the 1600cc engine in Beales's Beetle blew a piston and that was that. Beales was obviously amused, this author obviously was not. (Photo: David Burdon-Bailey)

flag on a number of international rallies including the RAC and the Welsh putting up creditable performances in his virtually standard 1600cc 1302S. On the 1974 Mintex Rally, he and co-driver, Dennis Abbott put up a splendid performance to finish second in the 1600 class again, using the standard 1302S. Dave's enthusiasm for motor sport is and always has been unquenchable and he has competed in a wide variety of events including circuit racing and trials at the helm of a Beetle, beach buggy or Type 3 'notchback'.

During the 1980s, Lucas became so excited about the prospect of competing in the newly-introduced Classic Saloon Car Championship that he went out and bought a Beetle without delay but his excitement was short-lived because, after just a few races, some kind soul jumped behind the wheel of the car which was parked outside Dave's house and he hasn't seen it to this day. Lucas thereafter threw himself heartily into the task of organising the now-defunct Birmingham Superprix. But, I digress.

The other privateer who performed great things with Beetles during the twilight years was the Oxfordshire garage proprietor, Francis Tuthill, a long-time Beetle and Porsche addict who, on his own admission, can rarely resist a real challenge. Francis has also competed in a variety of events in Beetles over the years but his greatest epic was the 1977 London-to-Sydney Marathon rally for which, he used a 1302S, just one of several Beetles in his collection.

In many respects, the 1977 event was even tougher than the 1968 'Sydney' but Francis and his navigator, Anthony Showell went well prepared stuffing the car with every conceivable spare part including an engine. After several weeks of hard driving against the clock and having to suffer the nightmare of performing major repairs to the car on the side of the road, Tuthill brought his trusty machine home in 36th position whereas another German entered Beetle driven by Jeandot and Koch finished in 17th.

Martin Southwell from Bristol enjoys a quiet moment on the Historic Rally Bristowe, a road rally that places the emphasis on navigational skills rather than speed.

The Volkswagen 'Notchback' is a very different animal from the Beetle but has scored a number of successes in both national and international events. Bill Bengry was the first to use one and won a round of the 'Motoring News' Championship in a 1500 in 1962. This is Perry Andersson at Prescott on the 1992 Charrington's RAC Historic Rally.

Tuthill took the same Beetle to 56th position on the 1979 RAC Rally but, had a rather special weapon being prepared in his Banbury workshops for future events. Never one to let the grass grow under his feet, he took one standard 1200 Beetle and set about modifying it for the national championship.

Disc brakes were fitted to all four wheels, the suspension was considerably stiffened up and a fuel-injected 2.4-litre Type 4 engine was shoe-horned into the 'business end'. With no less than 174 bhp instantly available under his right foot, Tuthill gave several Escort drivers a taste of their own medicine scoring a sensational fourth overall on the 1980 Russek Memorial Rally. Francis used the car to good effect on several occasions reporting that fuel-injection, rather than carburettors, was a great advantage in extracting more power from the engine.

Because Volkswagen stopped producing Beetles in Germany at the beginning of 1978, the car's time in international competition was running out. Homologation finished at the end of 1983 and a number of Beetle nuts turned out to watch the 1302S of the Austrian pairing of Harrach and Gottlieb competing in the RAC International of the same year. Unfortunately, the car retired in the early stages after the engine's cooling fan sheared off, an almost unheard of occurrence and that was that.

Andersson's 1500S negotiates the esses at Prescott, a notoriously tricky series of bends but thankfully, they didn't catch him out.

However, because Beetles are still made in Mexico to this day, homologation was restored and, at the time of writing, the last appearance of a Beetle in an international rally was in 1992 when, once again, Francis Tuthill entered a Beetle (or Fusca) for the 1992 RAC. On this occasion, Francis sat in the passenger seat while his young son, Richard took the wheel. A virtually standard 1600 torsion-bar car, they finished in 96th position overall but, at least they finished.

At the time of writing, the Tuthills are hoping to enter the same car for the 1993 RAC but, once again, there is a question mark hanging over homologation. Only time will tell if time really has, at last, run out for the Beetle on the international rally stage.

Assuming that homologation is granted, the Beetle will be the only car still made (apart from the Morgan and the Mini) that is eligible for both modern and historic events, quite some record when you consider that the first production Beetle rolled off the Wolfsburg assembly lines in August 1940.

CHAPTER TWO

On the right track

If you've always thought that Walt Disney's film 'The Love Bug' about Herbie, the cheerful Beetle with a mind of its own was a little far fetched, then perhaps it is time to think again because Beetles really can and often have beaten much more powerful cars on the race track.

In particular, George Reynolds of Australia became especially proficient at embarrassing Jaguar drivers with a 1300 Beetle in the mid-1960s but in Britain, Europe and the USA, it is not untrue to say that the Beetle was never thought of as an ideal basis on which to make an out-and-out circuit racer.

One of the reasons for this is arguably because Volkswagen's management did not feel that the car's image was suited to the fast world of motor sport and instead, gave limited support to Formula Vee single-seater racing cars which were built around the Beetle's mechanical components.

Formula Vee, which originated in America, was intended to provide a low-cost starter formula for young talent on their way to the top. As the cars used 1300 Beetle engines and torsion-bar suspension, everything was kept nice and simple and enabled owner-drivers with limited mechanical knowledge to build and prepare their own cars.

As the cars were very light in weight, it didn't particularly matter that the engine output (at around 60 bhp) was very low because, in a straight line, the little cars were easily as fast as a modern Golf GTi flat out.

The sport quickly developed and by the mid-1960s had spread to several countries in Europe, South Africa and Australia. By 1970, these single seaters were being tuned to give 95 bhp and a number of people, including Gerhard Mitter, had been particularly successful in European Championship events.

However, broadly speaking, Formula Vee has attracted motor racing enthusiasts over the years rather than typical Volkswagen folk and as a Formula, its success has been very much overshadowed by Formula Ford. Even when Formula Vee was superceded by Super Vee and more powerful 1600 engines, Formula Ford continued to be thought of as the best proving ground for up-and-coming youngsters with their sights firmly set on Formula One.

Despite the onslaught of Formula Ford, today's Formula Vee scene continues to attract a healthy number of followers on both sides of the guard-rails but whereas it has not brought dyed-in-the-wool Beetle people out of the woodwork, the recently inaugurated Beetle racing championships most certainly have.

Since the 1960s, a number of Beetles have been used in various saloon car

Volkswagen Motorsport supported Formula Vee single-seater racing but never officially recognised the Beetle as a potential 'sports' car. Here, a number of Beetle-powered Vees line up in the paddock for a race at the old Nurburgring circuit. (Photo: Volkswagen Press)

If you think the idea of 'Herbie' beating more powerful cars on the race track is ridiculous, it's time to think again.

Thanks to Shaun and 'Olly' Hollamby, Britain now has its own Beetle racing championship. This is Tony Cook at full chat at Cadwell Park.

Julian Lock is by far the smoothest, fastest and most talented driver in the Big Boy's Toys championship having won the 1992 title and the Brands Hatch Superprix.

Steve Johnson of ITV's 'Motor Mouth' fame has an interesting moment but displayed masterly skill in recovering from this high-speed backwards slide.

championship races throughout the world but have been always pitted against other marques. Famous names are proud to remember their days behind the wheel of a Beetle including Emerson Fittipaldi who once raced a demon twin-engined car in South America and Peter Sauber (whose Swiss-based Mercedes outfit won the 24-Hour car race at Le Mans in 1989), but only in the last few years have Beetles been used in their own 'one-make' championship.

Thanks to the Germans, an all-Beetle championship was first launched in 1989 and has subsequently gone from strength to strength in attracting large crowds of spectators to the various events held throughout each season.

The Käfer Cup which started up in Germany in 1989 is now one of that country's most successful national series and, as its title suggests, caters exclusively for Beetles and their drivers. There are several classes for which the cars are eligible from standard unmodified cars to 'breathed-on' racing machines and apart from circuit races, each season also includes hill climb and slalom events in true German tradition.

Sponsored by the German Volkswagen magazine 'Gute Fahrt', the series has gone from strength to strength and because of the relaxed restrictions on power output for the top modified class for Type 4 engined cars, the Germans have demonstrated that the Beetle can perform on the circuit as well as more modern racing cars. Indeed, in a recent back-to-back track test published by Gute Fahrt between a race-prepared Porsche 911 and one of the Käfer Cup Beetles, the performance figures showed that the cars were evenly matched but this kind of Beetle power does not come cheap.

A typically modified Type 4 engine 'bored out' to 2.5-litres and encouraged by a pair of Weber 44 carbs will willingly punch out over 200 bhp and offer spirited drivers the chance of whistling around the Nurburgring at speeds of up to 130 mph and more but, for each additional mile-per-hour over the magic ton, is thought to be roughly equivalent to the number of letters you have to write to your bank manager to persuade him to allow you to continue the rest of the season.

Here in Britain, we now have our own Beetle racing championship which began in 1992 and is sponsored by the independent Beetle specialists, Big Boys' Toys. Clearly inspired by the German Beetle series, it was the brainchild of Shaun Hollamby and his father Keith who run Big Boys' Toys.

Both Shaun and Keith (known to his friends as Olly) are well-known in British Volkswagen circles and both have had considerable experience driving a variety of racing cars in national championships. Shaun was particularly successful in Formula First single seaters but eventually turned his attentions to organising the Beetle cup and, in its first year, secured a Beetle grid for 10 races held at Brands Hatch, Oulton Park, Cadwell Park, Donington Park, Snetterton and Castle Combe.

Not surprisingly, the new series attracted a great deal of media attention. It was after all, the first time Beetles had taken to British racing tracks in any numbers and ordinary everyday motoring folk just love Beetles.

Right from the start, the Beetle Cup couldn't put a foot wrong. The cars were beautifully prepared and looked utterly gorgeous and because each car was built to the same specification, the winner would not be judged by the size of his bank account as has happened so many times previously in motor sport. Instead, this was a competition that, in the fullness of time, would discover true driving talent.

But that is not to say that those who habitually qualified and finished way down the field were talentless because one of the great things about this series, is that it was also designed for enthusiastic Beetle 'nuts' who wanted to have fun and experience the joys of circuit racing. Many competitors have expressed the view that, for them, taking part in their favourite car in their favourite sport is considerably more important than winning.

Throughout the 1992 and 1993 seasons, each race continued to attract a healthy crowd of spectators for the simple reason that the competition is close and exciting. For those interested in watching thrills and spills, the Beetle Cup comes a close second to the British Touring Car Championship. As more and more people got to grips with the inherent tendency of the Beetle to oversteer, the racing was fast and furious. There were famous scraps which ended in disappointment for some and elation for others but it has always been and continues to be all good clean fun.

At the end of 1992, Julian Lock established himself as a clear and worthy winner, his smooth driving style and natural ability leading to an outright victory in both the championship and the Brands Hatch Bug Prix.

In trying to create a high-profile series, Shaun Hollamby succeeded in attracting a number of well-known personalities to drive including the well-known motoring

Motoring journalist and presenter of the BBC's programme 'Top Gear' Chris Goffey threw himself into Beetle racing with great enthusiasm but, like most of the other competitors . . .

. . . experienced an occasional altercation with the tyre wall.

Peter Kays never provides anything less than good value with his exuberant driving style.

Even 'Autosport's' Marcus Pye was tempted away from his editorial desk to take part in a round at Brand's Hatch. In this shot, he is driving the Hollamby-prepared 'works' car at around 85 mph through Paddock Bend.

Glenda McKay, star of ITV's long-running soap, 'Emmerdale' is a welcome guest at selected events.

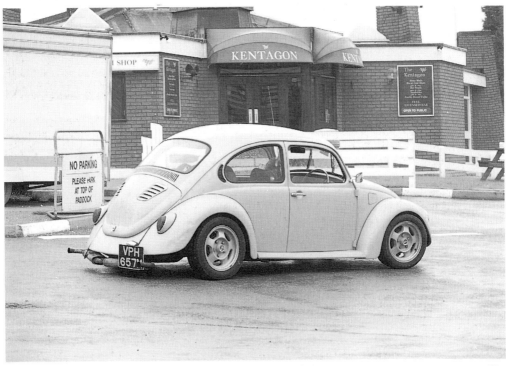

Parking a Cal-looker outside the Kentagon at Brands Hatch is the ultimate in 'super-cool'.

The action, particularly at Brands Hatch is always close and spectacular.

Beetles are renowned for being easy to maintain. You don't have to be a brilliant mechanic to keep even a racing Volkswagen in tip-top order.

Engine size in the Big Boy's Toys Cup is restricted to 1641cc, sufficient to propel a Beetle up to a maximum of 110 mph depending upon the circuit.

Grant Cassidy is one of the sport's great enthusiasts and characters. His black Beetle was something of a wreck when he acquired it but built it up into an immaculate racer. The paintwork is genuine London taxi-cab black.

journalist and presenter of the BBC's 'Top Gear' programme, Chris Goffey who has shown that he's more than up to the job of conducting Beetles at high speeds even if over-exuberance on the odd occasion has ended with an escapade into the scenery, Steve Johnson, presenter of the children's programme, 'Motor Mouth' and Glenda McKay, star of ITV's long-running soap, ' Emmerdale'.

Even the 'Autosport' motoring writer, Marcus Pye has been tempted away from his desk by the lure of the championship but, at the time of writing, (halfway through the 1993 season), it is Julian Lock again in the lead for the championship hotly pursued by Mark Sumpter and Simon Howarth.

Other notable performances have come time and again from John Aitkenhead, Peter Kays, Jason Winter, Dave Alderson, Phil Horne, Olly Hollamby himself (still capable of showing a clean pair of heels to the younger chaps), Neil Birkitt and Richard Smart with Grant Cassidy never giving anything less than value for money.

Grant Cassidy is one of the sport's 'characters' and what he lacks in finesse is made up for during each race by determination and bravado. His car, a self-prepared black Beetle with a prominent red stripe was once a rusted out wreck which required a great deal of welding work to merely make it look like a Beetle but Grant tackled the job with customary enthusiasm, engaged the services of a friend who performed a fine job of repainting the car in genuine London taxi-cab black and went racing. A place on the winner's rostrum has so far eluded him but the crowds appreciate his unique presence nonetheless.

Now supporting the British Touring Car Championship on the annual calendar, this high-profile popular series is, paradoxically, one of the cheapest ways to enjoy proper motor racing in the 1990s. And for those who feel sufficiently inspired to take to the track, it is worth looking at the cost of getting started.

Firstly, you need a Beetle. Depending upon its condition, a reasonably rust-free car in good running order with an MOT is going to set you back around £1,500. If you can get a good car for a lot less with a broken engine, so much the better because the standard engine will have to be removed anyway.

Under the current regulations, you have to buy all the bits and pieces to convert your road car to a racer from Big Boys' Toys. For the princely sum of £1,990 (plus VAT), you get a complete kit comprised of a six-point rollcage, tuned engine, racing seat, Kadron exhaust system, a set of four Spax shock absorbers, fire extinguisher, electrical cut-out switch, racing seat belts and a pair of overalls. To ensure that no-one gets an advantage by using special tyres, Dunlop D8 185/55 × 15 rubber is compulsory.

The choice of wheels is not restricted other than by size which can not be any wider than $5^1/2$J. Most competitors favour Cyclone alloys because they are not only very light but appear to be immensely strong, an important consideration when you take into account the formidable loads imposed upon them under normal racing conditions.

Built specially by Big Boys' Toys, the engines are sealed 1641cc units developing approximately 70 bhp at the rear wheels and enable the cars to reach speeds of up to 110 mph depending on the circuit. Each power unit is fitted with a 120 Engle

Phil Horne at the wheel of his beautifully turned out blue car.

Andy Halberry, a smooth and polished driver who quickly came to grips with the Beetle's inherent tendency to oversteer.

camshaft, an uprated Melling oil pump and a lightened flywheel and naturally, the crankcases, cylinder heads and pistons and barrels are brand new rather than reconditioned items.

In the interest of keeping costs low, the standard gearbox must be retained but suspension lowering is allowed and a certain amount of discretion must be exercised by the owner in this department. Set the ride height too high and you will be at a huge disadvantage in the corners. Set it too low at the rear and a wild degree of negative camber will decrease the available grip from the tyres.

Thus far, if you have concentrated on doing most of the preparation work yourself, it seems likely that you will have spent little more than £4,000. On top of this, you will have to buy a crash helmet and considering what it protects, it is worth spending as much as you can afford. Bank on spending £150 on a decent 'skidlid'.

You will then have to decide whether you are going to drive your car to each meeting or you are going to put in on a trailer and tow it behind another vehicle. The former route will save money but will make it difficult to get home at the end of the day if you damage the car. Stay out of trouble on the track (not always easy) and the need for an additional vehicle and a trailer will disappear.

The majority of competitors budget for around £100 – 150 per meeting which takes account of the cost of petrol, insurance, hotel (a tent and camping gear is the traditional way of saving money here) but part of that expenditure can be recouped with prize money. The top 20 finishers in each event get £50 in their pockets for their troubles. With 10 races per season, you get £500 back which has got to be good news.

Naturally, you will have to invest in a competition licence and attend a one-day course at an approved school of motor racing which should set you back less than £200 but, it's money well spent considering what you learn about the various high-speed driving techniques.

So, for less than £6,000 including the cost of the car and its preparation, you can have a whole season's motor racing. It still sounds expensive? Well, compare it with other forms of motor racing. A top professional outfit determined to be successful in Formula Ford can bank on getting little change from £70 – 100,000 for just one season. Jump up a few leagues to Formula 3000 and you'll have to find three times that amount merely to stay with the pack.

Compare Beetle racing with game shooting, salmon fishing or flying a light aircraft and it will soon become apparent that the former provides more adrenaline per pound note (sorry, coin) than just about anything else these days.

"The Beetle Cup has achieved exactly what we set out to achieve," says Shaun Hollamby. "Beetle racing provides the man in the street with an opportunity to get on to a racing circuit at grass roots level. Because there aren't vast sums of money involved in the series, the pressures to do well that are so obviously present in other forms of motor sport, just do not exist.

"All the competitors are very friendly people who help each other out at meetings by lending a hand where it is needed. There is friendly rivalry on the track and good sport from good sportsmen and women.

The front wing of Peter Kays' car has become detached as a result of contact with another car but, being a bolt-on bolt-off panel, the damage is easily rectified.

The action at Brands Hatch in 1992 was so good that even Bob Shaill, arch-defender of the vintage VW faith, turned up in his unique and oh-so sporting Stoll Coupe.

The lunch break provides ample time to sort out the car before racing commences.

A road-going Cal-looker is an ideal basis on which to start preparing a car for the Big Boy's Toys Cup.

Mark Saines' Beetle is arguably one of the best turned out Beetles.

Activity in the pitlane before a race but the atmosphere is friendly and relaxed.

Julian Lock is often on his own way out in front . . . which must be pretty lonely for him.

Steve Johnson and Grant Cassidy battle it out.

Neil Birkitt, editor of 'Bug Power' and assistant editor of 'VW Motoring' magazine is rarely far away from the front of the pack but has yet to find the formula for an outright victory.

British Beetle racing is about the cheapest way of getting on to a racing circuit and having some serious fun. The cars look the part and go superbly well and all for between £100 – 150 per race.

"At present, we have no plans to increase the size of the series by opening up classes for larger-engined Beetles as they have done in Germany. Costs would escalate and one of the reasons for the success of what we are trying to do is that costs are low."

Beetle circuit racing in both Germany and Britain has done a great deal towards helping the recent revival of interest in the Beetle on both sides of the English Channel. Beetles are also raced in America and with some success but there is, as yet, no national series specifically catering exclusively for them.

Changing Into Top Ghia

It would make for a pretty dull world if all Volkswagen fanatics took to the tracks in a Beetle which is why not all of them do. Back in the early 1980s, Dr. David Enderby, a London-based anaesthetist bought what started out in life as a perfectly harmless 1960 Karmann Ghia. He liked the look of the car (most of us do) and set about developing it for racing in the British Thunder Saloon Championship, a series created for highly modified saloon cars with engines churning out perfectly outrageous quantities of power.

David's car certainly looks like a Karmann Ghia but that's where any resemblance to the original Osnabruck-made car ends for this is a purpose-built racer that simply eats Cosworth Sierras and the like for breakfast.

To build the car, the conventional Volkswagen platform chassis was substituted for a complete Tiga 2000 Sports chassis and the bodywork was specially constructed from Kevlar except the detachable front and rear panels which were made separately from GRP.

Rather than hanging the engine out in the tail behind the gearbox in Volkswagen fashion, Enderby's car is mid-engined as well and although it started its competition life with a 1,000cc Hillman Imp unit, it was soon thereafter to be powered by a 1300cc 200 bhp Cosworth BDA engine mated neatly to a racing Hewland gearbox.

In fact, by the time the car had been developed to this stage, there was little if nothing of the original VW remaining because even the badges on the nosecone and the steering wheel were hand painted in an attempt to prevent fans of the Beastie Boys pop group removing them. Remember that craze?

A regular class winner, David Enderby's Karmann Ghia was easily blasted up to 160 mph for which, according to David, you needed a steady nerve. Being an anaesthetist, Enderby is well used to steadying his nerves which is why his skill in conducting the Ghia was something quite out of the ordinary.

In all, the car cost around £10,000 to build and regularly recorded times in the region of 1 min 44 secs for a lap of the full Brands Hatch Grand Prix circuit — not exactly hanging about by anyone's standards.

Dr David Enderby's racing Karmann Ghia is based on a Tiga sports car chassis and has a replica body specially constructed from kevlar and glass reinforced plastic. The Cosworth BDA engine is sufficiently powerful to allow the car a maximum speed of 160 mph.

The only part of David Enderby's Ghia that has anything to do with VW is the roundel in the middle of the steering wheel and on the bonnet but even they were painted on by hand to prevent them from being stolen.

Beetle On A Shoestring

If, like most of us, you have considerably more enthusiasm for Beetle racing than the necessary 'greenbacks' to actually sign the form that allows you to drive into the paddock, consider the case of one-time Classic Saloon Car racer, John Harrison.

The Classic Saloon Car challenge came about in the 1970s for those who wanted to do considerably more with their old cars than drag them on the back of a trailer to one of the increasingly popular 'show-and-shine' events so beloved of those who prefer to spend money on wax polish rather than petrol and oil.

Initially intended for pre-'57 cars, the series was soon extended to include saloons made up to 1965. Jaguars, Lotus Cortinas, Anglias, A35s and Imps were naturally popular but John Harrison took the unorthodox route of using a 1961 Beetle for which, he paid just £20. It cost him a few bob to prepare the car for speed and safety but, even so, a £20 racing car has to be something of a record in this day and age.

Resplendent in its menacing black livery, John lowered the car all round by four inches in time-honoured fashion at the rear by rotating the torsion bars and at the front with adjusters welded into the torsion-bar tubes. Fourteen-inch (rather than standard 15-inch) wheels were shod with 175/70 Uniroyal tyres and the engine was increased in size to 1,285cc.

Under the regulations, there is little you can do to tune a Beetle engine for classic saloon car racing so John paid particular attention to engine balancing. The heads utilised larger-than-standard valves, a specially made inlet manifold, a lightened flywheel and an Ansa four-into-one exhaust system.

In all, the Beetle developed more than 70 bhp at the flywheel which allowed a respectable top speed of around 100 mph and an impressive 0 – 60 mph time of 10 secs, not enough to stay with the Lotus Cortinas let alone get ahead of them but John did finish the '88 season fourth in his class and won the McMullen Memorial Trophy at the same time.

To his credit, he also distinguished himself by driving the car to and from each event which speaks volumes for Volkswagen's legendary reputation for reliability. Unfortunately, no-one has subsequently followed John Harrison's example of using a Beetle for classic saloon car racing which is a pity.

CHAPTER THREE

Mud, glorious mud

Away from the world's well trodden rally routes and smooth tarmac' racing circuits, there is a vast array of competitive events at which Beetles and other rear-engined Volkswagens have excelled. They include off-road trials, autocross and rallycross to name but three and perhaps surprisingly, Beetles in particular, still figure high up in the results lists to this day.

These types of competition have, over the years, attracted a very different breed from those involved in the more traditional branches of the sport yet, Volkswagens continue to serve their purpose as a tool in which to have fun and achieve success.

Classic Reliability Trials, often cited as the oldest form of road rallying in the world, have been especially popular with Beetle owners for many years and if you've ever watched or participated in one such event, it will be obvious why. The Motor Cycle Club of Great Britain has organised a series of trials for both motorcycles and cars since the pioneering days of internal combustion before the First World War and today, the 'Exeter', 'Land's End' and 'Edinburgh' or 'Triple' continue to form the backbone of the Club's activities.

So, just what is a classic reliability trial? Well, if you picture in your mind, the steepest, roughest, tightest, most slippery hill you've ever seen or tried to ascend on foot, it is probably part of an MCC trials route. Of course, one hill on its own is no good but a dozen or so similar courses within, say, a fifty-mile radius is just the job and when you link them all together with a few public and not-so-public roads, you've got the makings of a good trial; a test of endurance, patience and skill for both man and machine alike.

This form of punishment is almost exclusively British which means that there is always an added ingredient to make things a little more interesting. That added ingredient comes in the form of bad weather and whether it comes in the form of torrential rain, snow or ice or a combination all three, seasoned campaigners consider it all part and parcel of the art of the trialsman.

Again, there are several classes depending largely upon engine size and bodywork and chassis modifications but in the four-wheeled categories, Beetles and beach buggies often make up the bulk of the entry. Naturally, each of the regular competitors have their own ideas on the most effective means to tackle each hill but, by and large, the general aim is to channel as much of the available power from the engine through to the 'road' *via* the rear wheel without losing grip. In other words, traction is at a premium.

With the weight of both the engine and gearbox over the rear wheels, Beetle and

Hillman Imp drivers are off to a good start but preparing a successful trials car will take more than reliance upon the standard layout of the mechanical components.

Basically, you must think of a trials car as the exact opposite of a circuit racer. Firstly, the suspension rather than being lowered, must be raised and to as great a height as is possible. Again, Sway-A-Away adjusters can be used at the front and the torsion bars can be rotated at the rear but in the opposite direction.

With a massive degree of positive camber, Beetles look awkward and gawky in this stance but it will at least give you the necessary ground clearance to avoid major damage to the underside of the car. As an extra precaution, strong sturdy 'sump' guards can be bolted underneath at the front to protect the suspension and, at the rear, to protect the engine.

Although not essential, a rollcage is a sensible precaution as are fire extinguishers and battery cut-out switches. Happily, accidents are very few and far between in trials but there is not much wrong in taking steps to minimise the inevitable risks associated with all sports. One additional piece of equipment which you will most definitely need is a strong tow rope attached to the front of the car and fitted in such a way that it can be released quickly by the marshals. Cars that fail to 'clean' a section are usually pulled out by a tractor and if your rope is not to hand, you will delay the proceedings quite unnecessarily.

Incidentally, the choice of tyres is limited to standard road-going items. Heavily treaded mud-and-snow tyres are not permitted and the only advantage any competitor has over another in this respect is in the choice of tyre pressures. Between six and 12 psi in the rear boots is favoured by most people but it does mean that you will have to pump them up to travel between stages. A small air-pressure gauge is therefore another essential piece of equipment to keep in the car at all times.

Deciding on what sort of engine to use is far from easy and few people will ever agree on this subject anyway because much depends on individual driving style.

One thing is for sure though and that is that the wild high-lift camshafts so beloved of every 'boy racer' prove to be about as useful as 'go-faster' stripes when it comes to climbing slippery slopes. Simon Woodall, a past Triple winner and one of the sport's most successful exponents in recent times reckons that a cam from a 1200cc Transporter is as good as anything in quelling masses of engine revs whereas many other folks have found that standard engines without modifications have brought them just as many medals and finisher's certificates.

One of the first people to use a Beetle for serious trials work in this country was Mike Hinde who bought his first one in 1953 soon after the first official imports started trickling into Britain. Initially, Mike couldn't afford a car at all and experienced Beetles from the passenger seat of Dr Robert Ball's Volkswagen on a number of road rallies.

Like everyone else who became heavily involved with Beetles in those days, Mike became hooked and after winning the rear-engine class on the 1957 Exeter Trial, his name has figured prominently in all sorts of events for which Beetles are eligible.

Indeed, Mike Hinde was the BTRDA National Champion trialsman in 1961,

Dave Lucas enjoys a spot of 'mud plugging' on the Chase Clouds in a borrowed Notchback.

Beach buggies are ideal for trials competitions until the weather turns nasty.

Simon Woodall and Barabara Selkirk in their amazing buggy. Simon is one of the sport's most enthusiastic campaigners and a past Triple winner.

James Massey with his late father, Mike, a brilliant driver and a man who personified everyone's idea of the true enthusiastic amateur.

The author with navigator, Mike Massey, competing on the 1984 Exeter Trial, an event on which a rowing boat would have been a more appropriate form of transport.

1962, 1963, 1965, 1967 and 1968 and collected no fewer than three Triples during the mid-1960s as well. But despite these successes, Hinde sees himself more as a rally driver. He finished in 10th position overall on the 1965 Isle of Man Rally driving a Beetle and scored numerous victories in restricted club events.

"During the 1950s and '60s, the Beetle was virtually unbeatable in trials events because there was virtually nothing else made at the time that had such good traction in bad conditions," he says. "You could always do well in a Beetle." Today, Mike Hinde is actively and enthusiastically involved in campaigning a 1957 Beetle in historic rallying.

A specially prepared car, it is fitted with a 1296cc Okrasa engine and although Mike complains that it doesn't give enough power (all rally drivers always complain that they have never got enough power), it didn't prevent him from finishing in sixth position on the 1993 Kerridge Historic Rally, a brilliant result considering the strength of opposition from the Lotus Cortinas, Mini Coopers and Healey 3000s.

On that occasion, Mike was co-driven by another famous and successful trialsman, Dennis Greenslade whose outstanding achievements at the wheel of a Beetle have earned him more trophies and medals than anyone else in the long history of the sport.

Dennis started his illustrious competition career in Beetles way back in 1971

Dennis Greenslade is about to get wet on the 1992 Allen Trial. (Photo: John Gaisford)

A ford like this is no joke unless your engine is well protected against water.

Mike Hinde scored a class win on the 1957 Land's End Trial. Mike was one of the first people in Britain to use a Beetle for competition work. (Photo: Hike Hinde)

You need plenty of nerve to climb a hill as steep as this even in a beach buggy.

when, as he says, he wasn't as comfortably off as he is now. "I bought a Beetle because I wanted a reliable car for both classic reliability and production car trials," he says. "I had also used Hillman Imps in competition but discovered that their transmission systems are weak and have now been driving Beetles for more than 20 years."

Despite owning a number of other cars, both ancient and modern, Dennis Greenslade maintains to this day that there is nothing he enjoys so much as his Volkswagens. Depending upon your point of view, his success makes for pretty depressing reading because to date, Dennis has no less than six Triples under his belt which he won in 1971, 1973, 1979, 1990, 1991 and 1992.

This year, he is attempting to win his fourth successive Triple something which no-one else has ever achieved. Dennis Greenslade can also add to his list, 13 consecutive first class awards and five consecutive class wins and despite brief love affairs with other marques, has always returned to the trialing fold with a Beetle. "Recently, I thought it would be a challenge to have a go in a Porsche 911 but the car wasn't as successful as I had hoped," he says. "Basically, it was too heavy, a good deal less agile than the Beetle and a lot more expensive to run. With a Porsche 911, you are constantly throwing money at it so, inevitably, I returned to Beetles."

Surprisingly, Dennis Greenslade owes much of his success not to a specially prepared car but to a Beetle which is little modified from standard.

His current 1300 mount has had its suspension stiffened and raised; but not too much as Dennis reckons that a Beetle on stilts doesn't handle properly — "With too much positive camber at the rear, you don't get much grip," he says. The engine sports a brace of Dellorto carburettors and a tuned Kadron exhaust system whose single-pronged tail pipe is swept upwards out of harm's way. In true trials fashion, he has fitted a spare wheel or two above the engine lid for the simple reason that any additional weight at the rear improves traction.

There is no rollcage because Dennis maintains that Beetles are strong enough to survive even a major roll without one, a notion borne out by early trials at Wolfsburg when test cars were deliberately thrown end-over-end down mountain slopes, brutal treatment that resulted in little more than panel and paint damage.

He has however, taken great pains to ensure that the underside of the car is well protected with a 'skid plate' and a sump guard. Even Greenslade's considerable skill is no guarantee against damage caused by large stones, rocks and deep gulleys.

In the world of classic reliability trials, there is little doubt that the 'Specials' such as beach buggies and the like, are on paper at least, the most likely winners. Their agility, handling and power-to-weight ratio makes them more suitable from the off as Simon Woodall and Dave Lucas have shown, (both past Triple winners) but Dennis Greenslade has achieved the vast majority of his successes in 'everyday' tin-top saloon cars which points inevitably to the fact that, once again, you need more than just a good car to go trialing.

"Driving skill and careful preparation is what success in a classic reliability trial comes down to," says Dennis. "You have to ensure that you understand the route card properly and the nature of the tests. You have to avoid making simple mistakes."

Incidentally, he also won the 1993 South West Championship and the VW Owner's Club Championship for the seventh time but, to his credit, has never become complacent about his success. "There is always something that can catch you out and there's always something new to learn," he remarks.

Dennis Greenslade's young son, Giles has also taken to trials in a Beetle recently and shows every sign of following in his father's footsteps. "When he beats me, I shall retire," says Dennis but, naturally, old Beetle drivers like old Beetles never retire completely. As mentioned above, Dennis has recently started a new career with Mike Hinde in Historic Rallying and with a combined record like theirs, the future looks very interesting indeed.

"We would like to do selected stage events," says Mike, "but, above all, we are keen to promote Beetles in as many competitions as we can."

Throughout the past four decades and now into the fifth since Mike Hinde started campaigning air-cooled Volkswagens in trials events, there are many people who have followed in his footsteps. Few have enjoyed the same success as Hinde and Greenslade for a variety of reasons but are worthy of mentioning just the same.

During the late 1950s and '60, few will ever forget the many performances of Martin Appleton particularly in production car trials because he was not only possessed of considerable car control but usually turned up to each event, come rain or shine, in a pair of leather shorts. When the rest of us were standing around huddled up to a mug of tea desperately trying to keep warm, Martin Appleton could always be seen walking each hill course prior to driving, in his ubiquitous shorts totally and remarkably oblivious to the terrible weather conditions.

In more recent times, Keith Vipond who was a Triple winner in 1984 has thrilled the crowds with his determined and precise driving style, a man who always seemed to be able to drive a Beetle in places where most people would think twice about walking. Again, Keith's success was the result of driving ability rather than expensive and complex modifications to his Beetle.

During the 1980s, anyone who wanted to seriously attempt intelligent guesswork as to the outcome of an MCC Trial had, in most cases, very few choices because apart from Dennis Greenslade, David Lucas and Simon Woodall, there was Richard Penhale. Richard has been especially successful in his beach buggy and his Type 3 Notchback but, with all these people, it makes little difference as to their choice of car for each event; they invariably finish right on top.

One of the really great things about the trials world is that it does not discriminate against age. Whereas circuit racing demands the fitness and mental alertness of a youngster, classic reliability trials require a different mental attitude and many older people can enjoy the same degree of satisfaction and success experienced by younger people. Geoffrey Margetts from Malvern, Worcestershire is just one such example. Geoff has campaigned both Morgans and Beetles for many years but has proved to be just as adept at organising events as he is in the driving seat.

Trialing is a demanding and fun sport which can be enjoyed by anyone with a car and a driving licence. It is a true amateur's sport. There are no big sponsorship

Mike Hinde lifts a front wheel coming out of a sharp hairpin. The year is 1959, when spectators still wore a collar and tie to sporting events. (Photo: Mike Hinde)

Mike Hinde on the 1968 Land's End but, unusually, still using cross-ply tyres. (Photo: Mike Hinde)

contracts to be signed, no money involved other than laughably small entrance fees, no motorhomes, no television cameras and no scantily clad 'dolly-birds' adorned with silk sashes to welcome the winners.

Instead, there are several hundreds of enthusiasts who share great comradeship and a common aim. Of course, it is competitive and there's a healthy degree of rivalry between each crew but you will not find any evidence of the intense and bitter political battles that have threatened other branches of motor sport in recent times and, should you consider taking up the sport, you won't find that you have to wade through a mountain of paperwork before you actually get into action on a stage.

And the technical rules are relatively relaxed. Provided you conform to the class rules, you can use virtually any car you want. For example, a few years ago, it occurred to the long-time Volkswagen campaigner, Dave Alderson that a short wheelbase Beetle would be better for tackling the hills than a standard one so he set about cutting several inches of metalwork from the middle of his Beetle.

The result was one exceptionally effective Beetle called 'Shorty'. What else? And Dave took it to victory on the Crackington League in 1989. In many ways, it is an ideal 'mud-plugger' and, in Dave Alderson the car has a most worthy *pilote* but, like so many Volkswagen folk, he is prepared to try his hand at anything and has had several personal triumphs driving another Beetle in the Big Boy's Toys circuit racing series.

Throughout the year, there are a number of trials held around the country in

The most successful trialsman of all time, Dennis Greenslade competing on the 1974 Conquest Trial in his 1302S. (Photo: Dennis Greenslade)

addition to the Exeter, Land's End and Edinburgh (The Triple). Most are one-day events and take place in remote countryside and the clubs responsible for running the various competitions spend a great deal of time ensuring that any damage caused to the hills by cars in the heat of competition, is properly repaired.

Not all routes and courses are as difficult as those run by the Motorcycle Club of Great Britain and some are a lot worse. It's a great sport but for those interested in taking it up, I would strongly recommend that you go out and watch an event or two before putting in an entry. Trialing will either confirm your long held belief in the virtues of staying on *terra firma* or cure your fear of heights for good. Incidentally, the names and addresses of the organising clubs appear at the end of this book.

Now, if trialing is a sport for motoring folk who like playing around in lots of deep, wet mud, autocross is for those who also like to play around in mud but, at much greater speeds. During a classic reliability trial, the maximum speed reached by the majority of competitors even on a timed section might be as low as 25 – 35 mph but it's altogether a different story in autocross.

In the days before motor car racing became highly specialised and before the rule makers, public relations people and marketing men created what motor sport is today, a number of small car clubs around the world, in America, Britain, Australia and several countries in Europe would gather more often than not, on a Sunday afternoon for a friendly 'thrash' around a grassy field in a variety of saloon cars which in most cases, doubled as 'shopping cars' at other times.

Autocross is a sport at which Beetles have also excelled, frequently beating other cars which, in theory at least, are more suited to the rigours of a grass track. In British autocross, the greatest and most successful driver of them all was Laurie Manifold, a crime writer and investigative journalist by profession. Laurie first took to the sport in 1954 and, up until his retirement in the 1970s, had collected over 200 awards in both national championship and non-championship events earning him not only the title 'Mr Autocross' but a record that has never been beaten to this day.

Today, Laurie Manifold lives quietly in retirement well away from his former life in Fleet Street and clearly remembers why he bought a Beetle and went racing. "Back in the early 1950s, I owned an MG TF and used it to go to and from work during the week and for sporting events at weekends. It was after all, the archetypal British sports car," he says, "but one night while returning to London from Portsmouth to meet a deadline, I was overtaken by a car which I had never seen before.

"The TF MG was a car that you could drive all day at 60 mph but would do 70 for five-minute bursts. Any more than five minutes and the engine would overheat badly and, on this occasion, I was booting it really hard when this funny looking saloon overtook me. What's more, I noticed that its driver was wearing a dinner jacket and wondered what the hell I bothered with a sports car for when I could be sitting in the unflustered comfort of whatever it was that had just gone past me."

The unidentified car, as it turned out, was a 1200 Beetle of course and Laurie decided that he had to have one. In fact, he had several over the years (mostly from

Colborne-Baber's garage) and became the man to beat at virtually all the major autocross events for the best part of three decades.

He was also the man to beat when it came to 'scoop' stories for the national press for Laurie's job was involved in working on major 'exposure' stories in the world of crime. "We bought stories from some of the most famous 'criminals' of the day and, if they got off," says Laurie, "I would whisk them away from the court, usually the Old Bailey, in my Beetle as fast as possible with the rest of the Fleet Street crowd driving as hard as they could to keep up with me."

Naturally, the Manifold road car doubled as the Manifold competition car and, with its 'hot' engine, modified suspension, wider wheels and close ratio gearbox, rival journalists hadn't a hope in hell of catching him. "What I did to get away from them was drive through the streets of London at a constant speed of 30 or 40 mph and, when I spotted a convenient turn to the left or right, I would simply take it without slowing down . . . the Beetle would go round corners perfectly without fuss but to watch some cars trying to do the same was really quite something else," laughs Laurie.

Quite often though, he was pulled up by the police because his cars usually included the letters 'VW' in the registration number. "They thought that the plates were made-up forgeries," he explains, "I used to get so annoyed for being stopped: it was a real pain in the backside on more than one occasion."

During the good ol' days when people involved with motor sport had little

A regular competitor in both trials and circuit racing, Dave Alderson at the wheel of 'Shorty', a car that has had several inches removed from its middle in an attempt to make it more agile in the corners. It works too.

It's best not to come to a halt up a muddy hill like this because if you do have to get out and push, you can bank on having wet feet for the rest of the day.

A pair of wheels fitted to the rear of the car help enormously in increasing traction.

The 1303 Beetle owned by Graham Brasier which Mike Hinde drove to many victories in the 1990 RAC Production Trials Championship. Using the same car, Graham was third overall in the championship the same year. (Photo: Mike Hinde)

A standard Beetle is ideal for trials work provided you raise the suspension enough to clear the mud.

The author pumping up the rear tyres of his 1500 Beetle during the 1984 Exeter. Some of the mud on the car was still in evidence five years later. (Photo: Mike Massey)

The dashboard of a typical trials Beetle includes additional gauges for amps and revs but an altimeter may be more appropriate for some events.

money (remember?) and helped each other out with the loan of tools, parts or just moral support, there was rarely any time to do things properly. Today of course, regular autocross competitors spend a great deal of both time and money testing and developing their cars but, in Laurie Manifold's day, everything was very different. "We all had full-time jobs and certainly tested our cars but didn't talk about it much," he says for Laurie and his co-conspirators used to sneak into Air Ministry property in the dead of night and fire-up the car with a view to running in a new engine. Naturally, autocross cars do not have lights and several torches lit the way.

These clandestine operations often involved several hours of high-speed running in but they did allow Laurie and his team to prepare the car properly before snatching a couple of hours sleep prior to an important competition.

On another occasion, it was decided by the team's patron that a new engine was needed. "I was introduced to an ace-tuner in Scandinavia," says Laurie, "and, always chasing a million bhp or so, I decided to import a special engine into the UK. The problem was that imports, at the time, were strictly controlled and there was no way I could legally bring a hot motor into the country."

However, where there is the will, there is a way, as the saying goes and Manifold, along with demon mechanic, Roy Wilson, decided that the engine they wanted which was actually in Finland, had to come to England by hook or by crook.

So, what did they do? The scheming little toads fitted Laurie's autocross Beetle

A rare sight indeed is this Volkswagen Brasilia competing on the 1980 Land's End Trial with Dennis Greenslade at the wheel. (Photo: Dennis Greenslade)

with a completely knackered engine (acquired for the princely sum of £15) and set off for Scandinavia on the ferry. According to Laurie, the engine was so tired that it actually struggled to propel the car and its two occupants off the boat and it finally expired just three miles after disembarking.

Of course, they knew exactly where to go to get a replacement power unit and within two days, Manifold and Wilson were heading back to England with the new competition engine firmly bolted in the back of the car. But what about the Customs and Excise people? Remember, import restrictions at the time were very tight.

"Oh, driving through customs was dead easy," says Laurie with a contented grin on his face. "We threw a load of mud all over the car as well as placing some advertising stickers on the bodywork and pretended that we had taken part in a rally in Sweden." They got away with their little scheme but justice was done in the end and what's more, was seen to be done as this precious engine, which had been set up to run in the cool temperatures of a Scandinavian winter, melted on its first outing at Brands Hatch.

SCAT is a name most Beetle people will have come across at some time or other. It's an American company that manufactures performance bits and pieces for VWs but, when Laurie Manifold was actively engaged in combat, SCAT was not quite so well known, especially in Britain.

This picture was taken to commemorate Dennis Greenslade's 100th trophy in trialing. By August 1993, the figure had risen to more than 300. (Photo: Michael Brooks)

Dennis and Tricia Greenslade celebrate their 1992 sporting year which included the ACTC, ASWMC, and VWOC Championships and a 'triple' Triple award. (Photo: Colin Higgs)

"A friend of mine was visiting America on business and I asked him to get me some special engine components from SCAT whilst he was over there," says Laurie, "but it just so happens that a man from Self Contained Auto Toilets tried to explain to my friend that they didn't exactly deal in Volkswagen components. Well, they wouldn't would they. Needless to say, he had looked up the wrong SCAT company."

Like so many people of his generation who took up the challenge of driving Beetles in competition, Laurie Manifold enjoyed nothing more than 'putting one over on the big boys'. "It always gave me a tremendous buzz to beat powerful cars like Porsches," he confesses. "Years ago, there was so much anti-Volkswagen comment in the national press that it was just great to prove them all wrong. We all had a lot of fun in those days too and one sight I shall always remember was that of Ken Piper making mincemeat of everyone in his little Messerschmitt."

One of the very few Fleet Street journalists who didn't seek relief from the pressure of work in the pub, Laurie vented his frustrations on the track but reckons he would have been next-to-useless as a tarmac' racer.

"I was always so tired that the bumps and yumps on an autocross circuit would wake me up whereas, pure track racing, which I tried a couple of times, just made me go to sleep," he says.

There was one occasion though when Laurie was a little more awake than he really wanted to be. During an interval between races, the car was checked over and

Mr 'Autocross', Laurie Manifold in full flight during the final of the Player's national championship at Silverstone 1967. (Photo: Laurie Manifold)

someone forgot to replace the petrol filler cap after the tank had been filled. Needless to say, the race itself saw Laurie making a hasty and uncustomary exit from the driving seat due to rather hot flames engulfing his legs.

It's interesting that virtually all the people who took part in one form of motor sport and another during the 1950s and '60s are agreed on one thing in particular. They will tell you that, above all else, it was great fun. "No-one took it too seriously in those days," says Laurie "but now, the pressures are fantastic. I used to tie a rope around my waist when I was competing just to hold my body in place on the corners. Beetle seats never did have very good lateral support and I used to slide about all over the place until I bought a bit of rope but you can't imagine trying to do that today. It just wouldn't be allowed.

"Back in the '60s, I can recall one chap bringing a four-wheel-drive armoured car to one meeting, a hellish and dangerous contraption which was allowed by the organisers to run on its own around the track. It drew the crowds, made us all laugh and it was great fun. Another competitor had a Porsche that he covered in velour cloth which was strange but again, it was just a bit of fun," he adds.

Just for the record, Laurie Manifold won the 1966 BTRDA Championship outright in a Beetle which his wife, Jean also used for transporting her Pugs to dog shows and in addition, won his class in the Player's cigarettes national championship in 1967 and '68. In all, he scored dozens of class wins in different championships and quite understandably, doesn't recall the details of each.

The multi-talented Dave Lucas competing in the Wildcam autocross, Staffordshire in 1977.

Someone forgot to replace the petrol filler cap on Laurie Manifold's autocross Beetle with rather inevitable results.

A fine study in how to drive a Beetle on a loose surface on the limit without coming to grief.
(Photo: Anthony Hollister)

Laurie Manifold was one of the few Fleet Street journalists who found an outlet for stress on the race track rather than in the pub. (Photo: Laurie Manifold)

Mike Hinde in action at an autocross event. This is what happens if you are unfortunate enough to land a Beetle on its nose. (Photo: Mike Hinde)

Manifold leads Bob Piper in the Player's Championship, 1967. At this stage, Beetles were virtually unbeatable in autocross. (Photo: Laurie Manifold)

Glass-fibre panels are absolutely great if you want to shed weight but don't last long if you happen to make contact with another car. (Photo; Laurie Manifold)

Laurie Manifold chalked up fastest time of the day with his 2.3-litre 1302S at a Stort Valley AC event in 1977. Note that the oil cooler is on the roof. (Photo: Godfrey & Horner)

A Mini runs wide and Manifold nips through on the inside to clock up another victory. (Photo: F. Scatley)

Today, he is no longer involved in motor sport of any kind having sold his last competition Beetle some time ago. His everyday transport is still a Volkswagen, naturally, but takes the form of an 'Umwelt' diesel Golf. His interest these days lies more with tractors which he uses for a variety of tasks around his large garden. "Fifteen forward speeds, lots of power and a maximum speed of 20 mph: plenty fast enough for me," he reckons.

Although Laurie Manifold was the outstanding driver during the hey-day of autocross, there were of course many others. Although he never won a national championship, 'Griff' Griffiths was both fast and spectacular and was one of the many people who, during the sixties, fitted his Beetle with a Porsche engine in an attempt to find more power and greater speed.

And there was also the Harrold brothers, Peter and Paul who, in terms of speed put the fear of God up just about everyone against whom they competed. Paul Harrold scored a well-deserved class win in the national autocross championship in 1971 and of course, Peter went on to compete in a fire-breathing four-wheel drive Beetle in rallycross.

During the 1969 season, it was Jim Taylor who was the star of the Player's No 6 autocross championship driving a formidable Porsche-engined Beetle. A class win, very nearly the championship in the Player's series, top honours in the BTRDA championship and a second in class in the Southern Jet sponsored series along with many other outright victories made Jim the darling of the crowds all season. Indeed. Tony Wilson writing in 'Autosport' magazine made no bones about the fact that Jim Taylor and his Beetle was the best driver/car combination of the entire season.

Ford Anglias, Escorts, Minis, Porsche 911s, Hillman Imps and home-built Specials formed the bulk of the competition during the late-1960s and early '70s but Jim Taylor's formidable Beetle beat them all. By this time, autocross had become extremely popular with competitors and spectators alike. The approach to the sport was suddenly different. Drivers became more professional, their cars were safer and better prepared and the competitive element became more intense. The racing was close but money was beginning to come into the world of autocross and, at the same time, honour began to go out of it at least where the big national championships were concerned anyhow.

Inevitably, the county motor clubs around the country continued to run their own events and still do but they were and are, low-key amateur events designed for the man in the street to have fun without breaking the bank. By the mid-1970s, autocross had declined sharply in popularity, not that there was anything particularly wrong with it. The events were usually well-run and there was always plenty of action but, during the early part of the 1960s, a new and some say more exciting sport sprang up which cast doubts over the long-term future of autocross.

Anyone who is now above the age of 35 will no doubt remember the terrible British winter of 1963. In that year, snow and ice lay on the ground for weeks on end and there was an awful lot of both. Along with a number of sporting events, the 1963 RAC Rally was cancelled because of the bad weather and, as a result, there was a large number of expensive rally cars and their disgruntled crews sitting around with nothing much to do.

So, some bright spark came up with the idea of holding a 'mini' rally at a single venue and, after a large show of hands, Brands Hatch was chosen as the most convenient track on which to have some fun. A course was mapped out which used parts of the then-Grand Prix circuit and a sizeable chunk of the infield as well giving drivers and spectators a taste of real rallying on different types of terrain within the confines of a small part of Kent.

The greats of the day including Timo Makinen, Erik Carlsson, Vic Elford and Paddy Hopkirk joined battle together, Makinen emerging as the eventual winner. It was all a lot of fun but didn't happen again until 1967 when, once more, the world's leading rally drivers descended upon Lydden Hill in Kent (now a test track belonging to McLaren International). The event, which was won by Vic Elford driving a Porsche 911S was also a great success but later that same year, the RAC International Rally had to be cancelled yet again, this time because of the foot-and-mouth epidemic and, a single stage event was quickly organised over the Bagshot training grounds to replace it.

At this stage, rallycross was almost indistinguishable from autocross but, as time went on, the various venues used by the rallycross fraternity were designed and specially built to include a number of different road surfaces including grass, tarmac', asphalt, chalk and gravel, real Beetle 'territory' and real rallying but held within a single stage.

Britain took the lead in establishing rallycross, its popularity quickly spreading to the European continent where the Dutch and Scandinavians were quick to catch on.

Rallycross quickly overshadowed autocross as the former progressed. It was (and remains) more spectacular and is both easy and cheap to televise. The 'great God' television is an important factor in establishing any sport these days and the presence of cameras right from the early days was instrumental in bringing large quantities of money into the sport from sponsors keen to gain long periods of product exposure at prime-time sports viewing.

During the mid-1960s, Griff Griffiths' autocross Beetle produced a perfectly respectable 100 bhp by virtue of its Type 3 1600 engine, twin Weber carburettors and high-lift camshaft. The car ran on 14-inch diameter wheels from a VW Transporter rather than the standard 15-inch items and suspension modifications were confined to adjustable shock absorbers and a stiffer anti-roll bar. Griff was successful but into the 1970s, the rallycross picture began to change for it was an era in which the all-conquering Ford Escort came to the fore and if you hadn't got one, winning became something of a challenge to say the least.

The days when you could take a slightly 'breathed on' Beetle out on a Sunday afternoon were gone for good. The works teams from Ford and Saab had arrived and Volkswagen's top brass in Germany were not about to start competing against them.

However, the Austrian Porsche importers mentioned in an earlier chapter whose team of 1302S Beetles had been so successful, dropped their rally programme and, for 1974, prepared two Beetles for Franz Wurz and Herbert Grunsteidl to compete in the European Rallycross Championship.

At that time, the rules governing the sport were comparatively relaxed and rather than struggling to squeeze 'tons' of power from a Beetle engine, the Austrian team substituted the ubiquitous 'oversized' competition power units for brand new Volkswagen Type 4 engines.

The Type 4 engine was inevitably designed along the same lines as the Beetle engine. It was air-cooled, had four horizontally opposed cylinders and came in 1700, 1800 and 2-litre guises but, had a considerably stronger crankcase, better oil lubrication and cooling properties including sodium filled valves and more scope for tuning.

Bored out to a full 2.4-litres, these cars developed well over 170 bhp and, after a season-long battle, Wurz claimed the title outright for himself. It was a remarkable success because it not only put Beetles well and truly back on the international competition map but, in winning the title, Wurz had beaten the very best cars from Porsche and Saab.

At the end of the season, Porsche-Austria closed its rallycross operation to concentrate on other matters but not all was lost for Beetle fans because, in the following year, a Dutchman, Cees Teurling drove a Porsche 911 engined Beetle to outright victory in the European Championship against even more fierce competition from factory teams.

Jean Manifold's champion pug, Willie is not especially impressed by Laurie's trophies. (Photo: F. Scatley)

That made it two international successes in as many years but for 1976, the rule makers delivered a bombshell insisting that, for the foreseeable future, all cars competing in rallycross had to use an engine originally destined for the car by its manufacturers. Such an engine could obviously be tuned but the new rules effectively did away with Porsche-engined Beetles in one fell swoop and even Beetles with Type 4 engines.

At that time, tuning components purely for Beetle engines were relatively few and far between and even for those rich enough to invest in the best, about the most they could hope for was a power output in the region of an optimistic 130 bhp. It was no good looking towards Wolfsburg for guidance because the factory just didn't produce the necessary 'goodies' and thanks to the rule makers, Stuttgart ceased to be of any use as well so, for a while, the Beetle virtually disappeared from the international rallycross scene.

However, by the beginning of the 1980s, things started to change and the future began to look a little brighter for the Beetle once again. In fact, the 1980s looked brighter for everyone. It was a new era in which massive media coverage would play an important part in boosting the sport to new heights. Television viewers demanded action. European economies were richer than ever before, members of the non-motoring public suddenly became switched on to the excitement of powerful cars in combat on an exciting multi-terrain circuit and the major motor manufacturers were quick to take advantage of the publicity to be gained from winning.

Off-road Volkswagen racing has not taken off in Britain, unlike these particular cars which 'yump' their way around specially built courses until something breaks or the chequered flag is held out.

It was the era of the Audi quattro, even more powerful Porsches, Saab turbos, Escorts, Fiestas, mid-engined Metros and Peugeots and Beetles, yet again. Thanks to sponsorship money, it was also a time when a successful privateer could work wonders against the works drivers if he also had the talent.

Engine power was increased from around 200 bhp in the mid-1970s to 500 and beyond by the mid-1980s. The cars were developed to include four-wheel drive, turbochargers, and multi-valve cylinder heads and if you hadn't any of these things, keeping up with the pack was out of the question let alone winning.

As viewers of ITV's Saturday afternoon 'World of Sport' programme will recall, rallycross suddenly became one of the most competitive and fastest sports around and for Volkswagen fans, it was particularly interesting because, there were Beetles to be seen regularly giving the quattros and Porsches *et al* a good thrashing.

Thanks to superb traction and almost hideous quantities of raw power, these cars on the tarmac' part of the Brands Hatch circuit along the pit straight to Paddock Bend were as fast as anything that had ever raced at the Kent circuit before including the awesome Group C sports racers and Grand Prix cars.

During the mid-1980s, it was the turn of the Scandinavian drivers to shine in Beetles, particularly Orjan Wahlund and the ultra-talented Mikael Nordstrom who, at the end of the 1985 European Championship finished in a most creditable fifth position overall.

Autotesting is very much a 'minority' sport nowadays but one in which a Beetle can still do well with the right person at the wheel. This is Clive Apperley driving his 1303S at an event organised by the once-great Herefordshire Motor Club.

During the late 1980s, the name of Peter Harrold surfaced once again, this time with a 400-bhp four-wheel-drive machine based on a 1303 bodyshell and although Peter was not to enjoy the success of yesteryear, his enthusiasm and natural driving talent certainly entertained the crowds. Peter even took his fabulous blue and white car to the Santa Pod raceway in the summer of 1989 and proved to be instantly competitive.

Over in Belgium, Francois Monten became a multi-championship winner in his turbocharged 1303 Beetle and was one of several people who came to Britain for the winter events to hammer home the message that Beetles not only provided great motoring entertainment with their sideways tail-swipes and great speed but that they were still competitive against much more modern machinery.

And you may well ask why a car that was designed more than 60 years ago is capable of beating modern-day 'supercars'. Superb traction thanks to the rear weight bias, the ability to change direction quickly for the same reason and a deep commitment by specialist tuning companies in providing high-quality tuning components provide us with some of the answers.

Unfortunately, no-one is currently using a Beetle for international rallycross on account of the fact that it has lost its homologation. That is not to say that Volkswagen Mexico couldn't be persuaded to homologate the car once again and give someone somewhere, a chance to prove the inevitable once again.

What a pleasant thought on which to end this chapter.

CHAPTER FOUR

Beetles in drag

By far the biggest and most important role played by the Beetle in motor sport today is in the increasingly popular world of drag racing, a quarter-mile sprint on tarmac' which owes its origins to the Americans. The fact that the Beetle was winning top-level competition well into modern times can largely be attributed to the development of the car by the Americans whose interest in quarter-mile drag racing and in long-distance, cross country Baja races, has influenced and shaped a whole new generation of Volkswagen fanatics whose energy and ingenuity in 'dressing up' the humble Bug for road and track alike knows no bounds.

The California-based tuning ace, Gene Berg began his love affair with the Beetle in 1956, making his own modifications to extract better performance from his everyday roadgoing or 'street' car. As he says, "Being married for only a couple of years and my first three sons already joining the family, I depended on this car for daily transportation so it had to maintain its reliability and economy."

Gene Berg's friends were impressed by his reworked Beetle and asked him to treat their cars to the same performance 'tweaks'. Between 1957 and 1961, Berg tuned Volkswagens as a sideline, opening his own Volkswagen shop in 1962 as Gene's Services based in Renton, Washington.

By this time, he had already experimented with Porsche 356 engines but quickly developed a number of 'hot' components of his own and, to prove that they worked, soon established himself as one of America's most successful drag racers.

"Our race program reliability speaks for itself and has provided more first place wins and runners up than any other single Volkswagen Beetle in history," he says. "We have developed race products that provide 10 to 15 years service, some in race applications with tests currently going on as, they still have not failed."

Similarly, Dean Lowry of the original EMPI company also started 'messing around' with Beetles at around the same time as Gene Berg and, like Gene, was totally committed to producing high quality components that not only worked but also offered long service.

Dean Lowry, Gene Berg and Joe Vittone are credited as the original instigators of many of today's racing products and technology, tried and tested over many years on drag and street-legal cars in addition to the specialised machinery that takes part in the long-distance Mexican Baja competitions.

For many years, it is not untrue to say that the established British motoring

As long as you have a roadworthy car with a current MoT certificate, the 'Run what ya brung' class is an ideal and inexpensive way to get started in drag racing.

A Karmann Ghia 'razor edge' lifts its nose getting away from the lights at a meeting at Long Marston.

With their lowered suspension, special body graphics and superb paintwork, Cal-lookers are popular street transport amongst the drag racing fraternity.

Santa Pod is possibly the only sporting venue in the world where a standard 30 bhp Oval will be warmly applauded for crossing the finishing line at 65 mph.

Dave Hersey's Beetle is a perfect and beautiful example of the Cal-look drag racer and it can also be driven on the road.

A purpose-built drag racer but fitted with the ubiquitous flat-four Beetle engine. A V8 Chevy might have been a better bet but some people just can't get away from Volkswagens.

fraternity and the European one to a lesser extent held a fairly stuffy attitude to drag racing and the people involved in this intriguing sport yet, great bodies like the Vintage Sports Car Club have held sprint meetings at several venues for many years.

And the only noteworthy difference between a VSCC sprint meeting and a drag event, apart from the quality of the cuisine served during the lunch interval and the number of ex-public school ties in evidence at the former, is the speed of the cars taking part. Drag racing cars are, by and large, considerably faster and much much more exciting. Anyone who has witnessed the ignominious sight of a typical vintage sports car (with exotic exceptions such as Bugattis, naturally) will know exactly what I mean. Yet, enthusiasts quite rightly get excited about both.

During the early part of the 1980s, the Volkswagen Beetle began to enjoy something of a revival. Of course, a hard core of Volkswagen folk had never allowed it to die even after German production finally ceased at the beginning of 1978 but, after that, a younger generation of people all over the world began to take an interest and before too long, everyone wanted a Beetle.

But not just any ordinary old Beetle because the Cal-look craze that was also started in the United States some years before was suddenly imported into Britain in a big way. Cal-lookers are closely linked to the drag racing world in America,

Trevor Atkinson's Karmann Ghia makes a refreshing sight and sound amongst all the Beetles.

And if you don't want to race your car, there's always the Concours.

Britain and mainland Europe and those people who identify and are associated with this second-time-around cult are to be applauded warmly for saving many cars that would have otherwise rotted in scrapyards.

In time, Cal-look found its way over to Germany, France, Switzerland, Holland, Belgium, Italy and so on and when in the mid-to late-1980s, it had reached almost epidemic proportions, a large band of drag racing enthusiasts got together and held meetings.

Today, Cal-look stands for considerably more though than merely altering the appearance of a standard Beetle because that is just a fraction of the story. For some, it is part of contemporary popular culture, a symbol of a new lifestyle, of an image or even a dream. It's about sea, sand and surf, art and music, fast driving and, in the modern idiom, it is about being 'super cool'.

Typically, a Cal-look Beetle (and no two are alike) is an individualist's car that is not only highly personalised but in many instances sets out to make a statement about its owner. Relieved of its superfluous brightwork, the bodywork is treated to a perfect paint job, the suspension is lowered front and rear and the engine, apart from being cosmetically dressed up will have been breathed on with plenty of tuning parts, mostly from America. Add to that, a mega-sound system, Porsche-

Dechroming, bright paintwork, lowered suspension and EMPI alloys are hallmarks of the classic Cal-look concours winners.

The Type 3 Fastback is a much underrated vehicle whose popularity has increased in recent times. Prices for these cars are still low and there are some real bargains to be had if you know what to look for.

The paddock at a drag meeting is always as interesting as the track itself.

style bucket seats and a new set of EMPI-type alloy wheels and you have the makings of the California-look.

The best Cal-look Beetles are works of automotive art which enhance the purity of the original design by eradicating the 'rough edges'. It is a subtle art form whose creators and followers are almost without limitations in their ability to develop the theme beyond that of the ordinary imagination.

And whereas in many other walks of motoring life, similarly loved, pampered and superbly dressed cars are trailered from one beauty contest to the next, the Cal-look crowd actually used their vehicles for the purpose they were originally designed; driving and driving hard.

Savour the unique atmosphere of a drag meeting at Santa Pod or the Avon Park raceway and even the most ardent, dyed-in-the-wool anorak devotee will soon find himself rushing to the grandstands to enjoy the spectacle of a burn-out.

Having evolved from virtually nothing over the past 10 years, the British drag racing scene is now so successful that the VW Drag Racing Club is in the happy position of putting on events exclusively for Volkswagens and one of the reasons for this is that anyone can take part.

There are several different classes for which Beetles and other Volkswagens can be entered depending upon their level of tune and preparation. Moreover, it

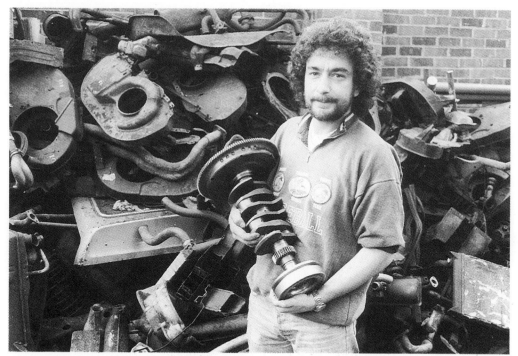

Luke Theochari of Terry's Beetle Services with a crankshaft destined for his car, 'Moody'. Able to withstand the stress imposed upon it by more than 9,000 rpm, this particular piece of kit costs well over £2,000.

is not necessarily the fastest and most powerful car that wins because thanks to the 'bracket racing' system used, victory depends on the consistency of each run.

Incidentally, Santa Pod, Britain's premier raceway is just about the only place in this country where a completely standard 30 bhp Beetle can cross the quarter-mile finishing line at less than 65 mph and receive a warm round of applause from the crowd, reinforcing the widely held belief amongst the fraternity in 'sport for all'.

At first glance, a Beetle (or any of the other air-cooled Volkswagens) doesn't appear to offer the ideal recipe for an out-and-out dash on a drag strip. The drag co-efficient of a standard car at 0.49 (roughly the same as a current Grand Prix machine) doesn't exactly make for a smooth passage through the air yet many of the top competitors are regularly reaching speeds of 130 mph and more.

Contrary to popular belief, driving a drag car in a straight line over a quarter-mile, involves considerably more than strapping yourself in and pressing the throttle pedal as hard as you can with your right foot. Brute force is certainly a factor in reaching the finish in under 10 seconds but, with 400 bhp bellowing out behind you, there's plenty of skill and concentration needed to counteract the inherent force produced by a crankshaft revolving at upwards of 9,000 rpm.

Gently as she goes. A beautiful Oval fitted with modern alloy wheels looks cute out on the track.

A good start is imperative when the lights turn to green.

Tyres as wide as these are great if you've got a powerful engine but a real handicap if you haven't.

In Britain, the cars, particularly in the 'modified' class have developed as quickly as the sport itself and over the past three or four years with formidable and regular contenders like Luke Theochari, Keith Seume, John Maher, Peter Englezos, Brett Hawksbee, Brian Burrows and many others, there have been some tremendously exciting season-long battles for top honours.

Each of these characters has his own ideas about how to get the best performance from the humble flat-four and in building their cars, have used many components specially built in America for the purpose in hand. In fact, it could be argued that in most cases, the cars have been so heavily modified that they have little of the original Wolfsburg 'tinware' left in place but one feels very much that, if Dr Porsche was alive today, he would far from disapprove of the many improvements made to his brilliant design.

To achieve really fast runs, it is widely acknowledged these days that fitting a turbocharger and nitrous-oxide injection is the way to go but John Maher's '57 Beetle is interesting because it continues to be mega-competitive without either.

At the end of the 1989 season, John, who is an ex-drummer with the 'Buzzcocks' met with an unfortunate accident whilst competing at the York raceway. His beautifully made green 'Oval' turned right at the end of the run whilst travelling at around 110 mph and completely destroyed itself leaving its owner not only a little

The interior of a purpose-built drag racer is necessarily austere. The rev counter is the most important instrument, not that there's ever much time to look at it and the rollcage is for safety. Superfluous trim that adds to the overall weight is discarded.

shaken and bruised but without a race car for the following season.

So, Maher made a decision to start from scratch and build himself a really special piece of kit. "Shortly after the accident, I went on an American tour with the band which enabled me to buy some of the special tuning equipment I needed," says John whose ambitious plans were for something different and unique.

Once installed back in his Manchester workshop, Maher's new car started to take shape. Firstly, he made a tubular steel chassis and replaced all the interior and floor panels with 1mm alloy sheet. The conventional torsion bar suspension was substituted for 'cut-down' MacPherson struts up front and ladder bars in conjunction with coil-over-shocks at the rear. Fibreglass was used for the unstressed external body panels in the interest of reducing weight.

The 2,165cc engine utilises 94 mm barrels, Wiseco pistons, a Gene Berg 78 mm crankshaft with a wedge-mated flywheel, 'Superflo' twin-port cylinder heads and 46 mm (inlet) and 38 mm (exhaust) valves made from titanium. Incidentally, the valves cost a cool £70 each and, as John says, "It's just as well that there are only eight of them." Fuel is fed to the engine *via* twin 48IDA Webers opened out to 51mm and the whole power unit drives through a Rhino 4-speed close-ratio gearbox.

Holes drilled in the wings allow the air pressure under the front of the car to escape which helps to prevent front-end lift at 130 mph.

Tony Duncan, Luke Theochari and Peter Englezos with 'Moody', a car that regularly swaps places with Keith Seume's 'No Mercy' for the title of Britain's fastest Beetle.

The author tries Moody for size and finds it more comfortable at 0 mph.

The idea is to warm up the tyres by performing a burn out . . .

. . . the car is then pushed into position . . .

. . . and finally hurtles from the start. From rest to 60 mph takes less than 2 secs.

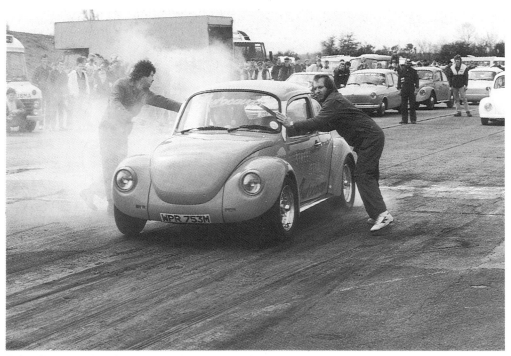

John Brewster has been particularly successful in Super Street with his 1303-based Beetle. Despite being road legal, John is only a couple of seconds slower over the quarter-mile than the cars in the modified class.

Brewster's car is a match for a 3-litre Porsche 911 in a straight line.

A smart Cal-looker on the left is pitted against a 'high-rise' Baja on the right. No, the Baja is not an ideal race car but everyone is welcome at Santa Pod.

There are no front brakes on the car but discs are fitted at the rear and the superb ultra-light Monocoque alloy wheels are shod with untreaded Goodyear Eagle tyres. The beefy rear tyres are nine inches wide and, to accommodate them under the wings, John has binned the standard driveshafts in favour of a pair of Henry's which are five inches shorter.

In its present guise, Maher reckons the car produces around 250 bhp and has already rewarded him with a personal best time of 11.5 secs at the July 1993 Santa Pod meeting which isn't at all bad considering this is a normally-aspirated machine. As a result of his efforts, the Maher Beetle weighs some 500 lbs less than a standard Beetle but was three years in the making and cost more than £10,000, a sum that takes no account of the labour and expertise John Maher lavished upon it.

"As it's fairly new, there is still a lot of work to do in developing the car," says John. "It handles quite well but there's some work to do on the engine yet if I'm to reach my target of a sub-10-second run."

By tradition, drag racers are given names and when Luke Theochari and Peter Englezos christened their Beetle, 'Moody', it was the result of a realistic assessment of the car's propensity for blowing hot and cold. Moody started its life as a 1974 1300 but when Luke and Peter acquired it in 1987, it was immediately treated to a new 1776cc engine and a close-ratio gearbox, sufficient for a best time of 14.89 secs on its first time out.

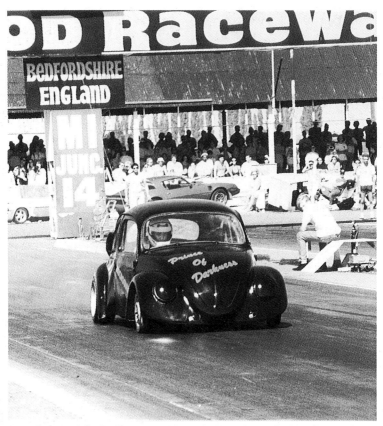

Paul Miller won the 'modified' championship in both 1990 and 1991 drivng the 1600cc 'Prince of Darkness'.

Next, it acquired a 2.1-litre engine and the times started falling. Since those days, the car has been substantially developed and modified to the point where it regularly swaps places with Keith Seume's car, 'No Mercy' for the title of Britain's fastest Beetle.

Before we look at Moody's all-conquering specification, a word or two about the genius of Peter Englezos. Peter is arguably amongst Britain's finest and most incredible Volkswagen spannermen and before the break-up of his long-time business partnership with Luke Theochari, was responsible for Moody's amazing performance and mechanical well-being.

Englezos became a Beetle fanatic when he was a small boy at school and spent all his spare time taking engines and gearboxes apart. Unlike many people however, Peter could also put them back together again. His interest turned into something of an obsession, as the truancy officer at Peter's local education authority will testify and, fed up with trying to persuade the young Englezos of the virtues of a formal education, he was expelled by the headmaster at the tender age of 15.

Needless to say, Peter never looked back and his extraordinary skills are now

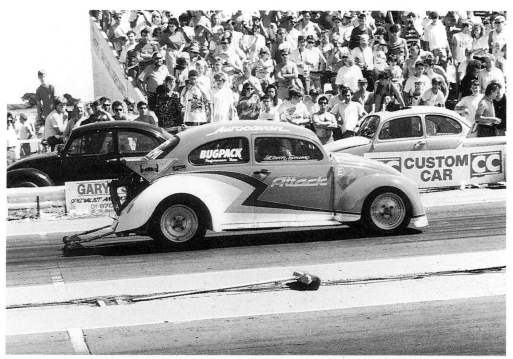

Editor of VolksWorld *magazine and the 1992 champion Keith Seume who has been instrumental in getting the British Volkswagen drag racing scene off the ground.*

Just warming up the tyres a little.

Peter Harrold's exciting four-wheel-drive Beetle was originally destined for rallycross but is seen here on the drag strip where its superior traction proved more than a match for the regular contenders.

Keith Seume's current mount, 'No Mercy' performs a burn-out prior to yet another blistering blast up the strip at Santa Pod.

If you run one of the top cars, there's always plenty of work to be done in the pits before and after a run.

Gary Angell's immaculate Beetle is a worthy contender in 'super street'. Note the stress imposed on the rear tyres under hard acceleration.

Ex-drummer of the 'Buzzcocks', John Maher in silent contemplation at the start of a serious day's racing.

much in demand. This author clearly recalls one meeting at Avon Park in 1989 when, during the morning qualifying runs, Moody was performing like an angry wasp with a bee under its bonnet and promptly threw a wobbly in the transmission. Peter and Luke were confronted with the choice of either returning home to West London or fixing the car so, during the lunch hour, Peter Englezos removed the rear body panels, the engine and the gearbox and split the latter with a view to investigating the problem.

A large crowd quickly gathered to spur their heroes on and, having located and remedied the transmission trouble, reassembled the gearbox, refitted the engine and bodywork and within slightly more than one hour, Moody was ready for the afternoon session when, amazingly, it recorded the fastest time of the day.

Peter and Luke won the championship in 1988 with Moody and continued to develop the car as time and money allowed. For the 1993 season it was running a 2447cc engine complete with a Pauter flanged crankshaft, Pauter pistons and barrels, Superflo cylinder heads, 48IDA Webers and an MSD engine management system incorporating a three-stage retard mechanism which allows a greater quantity of nitrous oxide to be pumped into the bores without the fear of high-speed detonation.

In this form, it pushes out 380 bhp and has, so far, managed a best time of 9.96 secs, unofficially the fastest ever quarter miler in Britain but unfortunately, Moody

Maher's car is radically modified from standard and not only uses a tubular steel chassis but a number of aluminium panels in the interest of saving weight.

was recently stolen from its garage in West London and although it was eventually recovered it had been stripped of all its precious competition parts.

For the 1994 season however, Luke Theochari has promised that Moody will make a comeback but will be very much faster than previously on account of the fact that he is currently building a 3-litre engine complete with a turbo-charger.

Endorsing the fact that consistency in drag racing is just as important, if not more so, than large quantities of power, Paul Miller took the modified championship in both 1990 and 1991 with his 1600cc Beetle nicknamed the 'Prince of Darkness'. Paul's car is about as low to the ground as is humanly possible and, even though its specification, has comparatively little of the sophisticated tuning equipment so dear to the hearts of other racers it goes well enough and the above-mentioned championship victories prove it.

The 1992 champion is 'VolksWorld' editor Keith Seume whose car, 'No Mercy' is arguably the most sophisticated and powerful of them all. Currently the fastest 'vintage' Beetle in the world with a best time 10.08 secs (October 1991), Keith's car is a right-hand-drive 1952 bodyshell mounted on a special spaceframe chassis.

Keith is correctly proud of the fact that the 2,165cc engine utilises many

After once turning suddenly into the guard rails at 110 mph, John Maher's car has one of the strongest rollcages in the business.

Volkswagen components including the cylinder heads which were reworked by KRE of America and are fitted with titanium valves. With its Wiseco pistons, Pauter crankshaft, 48mm Dellorto carburettor and a Rajay turbocharger, 'No Mercy', punches out an impressive 420 bhp.

Unlike John Maher's car, Seume's Beetle is fitted with disc brakes on all four wheels and has fully independent rear suspension. With its original split-window steel body, Seume confesses that the car is a little overweight but, with a top speed of around 140 mph, it's probably just as well.

Racing at this level is not only exciting but costly which is why the Super Street and Street classes are the most densely populated on the British and European drag scene. Both classes are for street-legal cars which means they must

One of the world's most beautiful drag cars, John Maher's Beetle is based on a 1957 bodyshell and took three years to construct.

Radically lowered and modified, successful drag Beetles have to be light and aerodynamically sound. This one has a rear wing mounted high above the rear window for enhanced stability at speed.

It certainly looks like a Beetle but the bodywork is made of glassfibre and the driving seat is positioned well back in the middle of the chassis. This car belongs to Brian Burrows, a future champion?

have a current MoT certificate and comply with the usual rules that affect everyday road cars.

To date, the most successful competitor in Super Street has been John Brewster who, unusually, has chosen to run a modified 1303 Beetle. John's impeccable preparation for each event is meticulous down to the last detail which is why his car is little more than a couple of seconds slower than the cars competing in the modified class. In fact, in a straight line, it is about equal to a standard 3-litre Porsche 911 over a quarter mile and was good enough for Brewster to win the championship class in both 1989 and 1990.

The Street class is for cars little modified from standard and provides an ideal forum for the owners of Cal-lookers to start racing.

Nothing too radical here but with the correct preparation and a powerful engine, even road legal Beetles can be quick.

Past Champions

Modified

1988	Luke Theochari/Peter Englezos (Terry's Beetle Services)
1989	Luke Theochari/Peter Englezos (Terry's Beetle Services)
1990	Paul Miller
1991	Paul Miller
1992	Keith Seume

Super Street		Street	
1988	Keith Seume	1988	no championship awarded
1989	John Brewster	1989	John Brewster
1990	John Brewster	1990	Travis Lawton
1991	Jim Bowen	1991	Mark Humphreys
1992	Jim Bowen	1992	Russell Fellows

It's not just Beetles that come in for neat customising treatment. The Volkswagen Transporter is an increasingly popular mount for Cal-look and drag fans alike.

CHAPTER FIVE

Buying, restoring and preparing a Beetle

For the uninitiated, buying a secondhand Beetle today is not usually the happy easy job it was a few years ago. There are many pitfalls to overcome if you don't want to end up with a pile of expensive trouble. As a general rule, it is best to spend as much as you can afford. A good car in the first instance could save you pounds on restoration work especially if you are not able or willing to carry out repairs yourself.

Because Volkswagen continue to produce Beetles in Mexico, would-be owners have a head start on someone who for example is considering the preparation of an Austin Healey or a Cortina because spare parts are still relatively cheap and plentiful.

And where spares are concerned, it is obviously better to go for a post-1967 'upright headlight' car rather than a pre-1967 six-volter. Various components for the latter are now becoming rare and in some instances very expensive so, you pays your money and takes your choice.

One of the reasons why it is becoming so difficult to find really good Beetles these days is simply that the majority on the market at any one time are now very old. It is as well to remember that even the newest of the German-built cars is now 15 years old and there are very few used 15-year-old cars that are not in need of major mechanical surgery.

In some cases, the bodies and chassis will have rotted badly and are best left alone depending of course on the purpose you have in mind. Another reason is that the Beetle in recent times has become a sad victim of its own success. An international 'cult' car which has enjoyed a massive revival in recent years, several have been exhumed from scrapheaps, given a cosmetic 'tart up' and have little to commend them other than a nice new shiny paint job.

During the mid-1980s, classic cars in general came under close scrutiny from investors who spent heavily in an attempt to make vast sums of money at a later date. Their market meddling saw prices for even quite mundane cars rise dramatically and unfortunately, the Beetle got caught up in the ensuing madness.

A number of unscrupulous operators seeing their chance for a quick buck jumped on the bandwagon and flooded the market with cars which, despite being unroadworthy in many cases, sold at a good price to unsuspecting Beetle enthusiasts who were eager to appear fashionable and chic.

So, don't get conned and remember that if you do buy a car that is in need of restoration work, there will be additional expenses later when you come to prepare it for competition purposes.

Incidentally, since the investors decided to move out of the classic car game recently, prices have stabilised once again and Beetles are now back at something approaching sensible money.

The best place to start looking for a good secondhand Beetle is in the classified columns of the specialist magazines because, on the whole, this is where you are likely to find an enthusiast's car that has been well cared for. It also pays to join your local Volkswagen club (there's almost bound to be one in your area) because it will not only be a useful source of spare parts but will also have members who are genuine experts willing to dispense invaluable advice.

Never be afraid to ask questions because someone somewhere will almost certainly be able to tell you exactly what you want to know.

Where body rot is concerned, Beetles are a known quantity. No part of the car is completely immune from corrosion but rust most commonly attacks the bottoms of the doors, the sills especially around the jacking points, the front and rear quarter panels, front and rear valances and the roof guttering.

The chassis has a tendency to rot away under the battery which is situated under the rear seat cushion and whilst you're probing in this area, it is important to check the condition of the rear inner wings, a common site for advanced rot in all Beetles.

Repair panels are available from specialist suppliers for all these areas except of course the roof guttering, the repair of which is always best left in the hands of an experienced craftsman.

On the whole, the torsion-bar Beetles are a good deal easier and less expensive to restore than the post-1970 MacPherson strut '02 and '03 range of cars. The latter are more complex and appear to be more prone to rot. However, the double-jointed driveshafts common to all the strut cars offer roadholding advantages and the decision to buy an '02, '03 or a traditional torsion-bar car must rest with the reader.

Which ever you decide, it pays to take a good long look at the condition of the underside of the car. Both types of suspension systems are extremely tough and durable but the front suspension uprights on torsion-bar cars have a tendency to rust through into holes which are actually difficult to find without close attention.

Torsion bars rarely break and it will be obvious to you if one has, front or rear but secondhand replacements are readily available. With the strut cars, pay particular attention to the underside of the spare wheel well and to the inner wings at the point at which the struts are attached. Both areas are popular sites for nesting metal beetles.

Mechanically, Beetles are about the toughest cars ever made. Pay little attention to the oft-heard phrase that air-cooled engines are living on borrowed time above 70,000 miles because it is simply not true. A well maintained car that has had its oil changed and tappets checked every 3,000 miles will last for more than double that mileage and beyond if driven sensibly.

Before starting the car and taking a test drive though, check the dipstick. Is the oil level correct and does the oil look clean? Is there evidence of oil leaks, does the

Having bought a Beetle, begin by stripping it down slowly and storing each component away carefully.

Rust commonly attacks the rear quarter panels and the only solution is to cut it out and weld new panels in.

Pay particular attention to the rear inner wings. Large holes like this are commonplace on old Beetles.

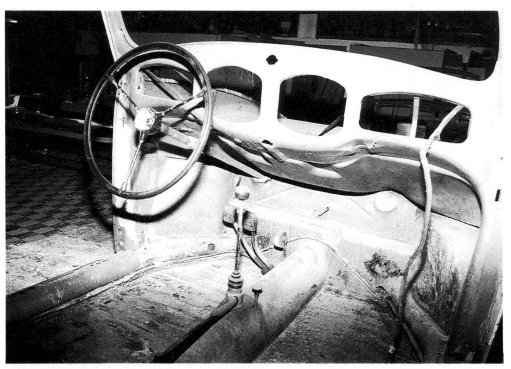

Don't be surprised if you spend a great deal of your time cleaning out dirt and grime that will have accumulated over many years.

engine look well cared for or is everything caked in grime? Has the carburettor been dripping petrol (evidence of a worn throttle spindle), is the fan belt horribly slack, are all the cooling trays in place?

Take a detailed look at the exhaust system. Holes in the heat exchangers and tail box will not only mean that expensive replacements will be needed but you will also get nasty exhaust fumes inside the car. If satisfied that everything at this stage is alright, drive the car and listen for nasty clonks and vibrations. A good car will have neither.

Common problems with tired cars are a tendency to wander from the straight and narrow which is usually an indication that the steering box or rack and pinion unit is worn, jumping out of gear which means that the synchromesh is worn or that the gearbox mountings are shot and a lack of willingness in the engine to rev cleanly and pull strongly.

A sound car will feel taut and lively. Worn piston rings, burnt valves, cracked cylinder heads and incorrect valve timing will lead to sluggishness and sloth. Obviously, none of these problems are terminal. All, without exception can be easily rectified but it is important to budget for them.

Incidentally, if the car you are considering is fitted with its original specification crossply tyres, make a note to change them as soon as possible to radials. Beetles aren't a lot of fun on crossplies as many a seasoned campaigner will tell you.

Having got this far, the next step is a test drive. Listen for clonks and vibrations when the engine fires up. There shouldn't be any at all. When you select bottom gear, leave the handbrake on momentarily and release the clutch. If the gearstick jumps about wildly, it is usually a sign that the rubber mounting at the front of the gearbox needs replacing. The mounting costs just a few pounds but replacing it involves several hours work.

It goes without saying that the brakes should be checked thoroughly. A car that pulls either to the right or left under braking is at best a menace and at worst, downright dangerous. Rectification of this problem is usually a matter of adjustment but if the discs or drums are warped which in most cases you will feel through the pedal under braking, replacements will have to be purchased and fitted.

And whilst out driving, have a good look at the windscreen as it is just in front of your nose. The recently revised MOT test requires that windscreens these days should be fairly blemish-free and if the one you are looking at isn't, be prepared for extra expense.

Buying a Beetle at the end of the day boils down to how much money you are prepared to spend. If you are confident of being able to carry out the restoration work and repairs yourself, a cheap car for a few hundred pounds may be your best bet.

If on the other hand, you haven't the skill, time or necessary tools to complete a successful rebuild, it's obvious that the safest route is to pay more for a good sound car in the first place. Good professional restorers charge handsomely for their services these days because the majority have expensive overheads.

Finding the right car for your purpose may well take some time so, be patient

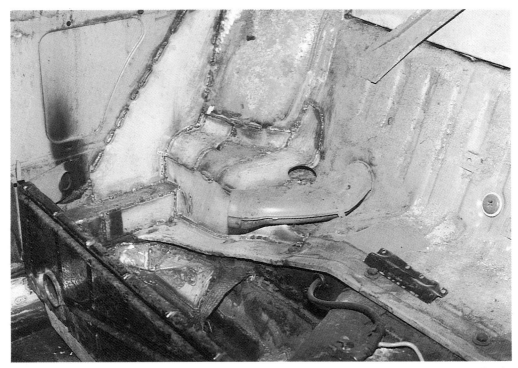

Welding in new metal as neatly as this demands time and patience so never be in too much of a hurry.

and don't be surprised if you reject the first 20 cars that are on your list. You won't be unique if you do. Should you decide to take the restoration route because you want to save money and because you love the idea of a challenge, write a list of the cost that is likely to be involved and double it as a precaution.

If you estimate a schedule for completing the work, treble it. An unheated garage with a bare concrete floor in the depths of a British winter is about as inviting as a ride around Silverstone on the rear aerofoil of Damon Hill's Williams.

Be realistic about your aims before you part with hard-earned cash. Allow your head and wallet to firmly rule your heart because there will be plenty of time for dreaming afterwards.

Beetle Price Guide 1993

Split-window	1945 – 53	£1,500 – £7,000
Oval window	1953 – 58	£850 – £3,500
1200	1958 – 67	£350 – £3,000
1300	1965 – 67	£350 – £3,000
1500	1966 – 67	£250 – £3,000
1300/1500	1968 – 70	£250 – £2,750
1302/1303	1970 – 75	£300 – £2,500
1302S/1303S	1970 – 75	£350 – £3,000
1200	to 1978	£250 – £2,750

Where the sills are concerned, the body will have to be removed if you need to perform major surgery. Here, new outer sills only have been fitted to this Type 3 Notchback.

The above is a rough guide and is by no means definitive. It excludes concours cars, special edition cars and cabriolets. Valuing almost any car is largely dependent upon the principle of supply and demand and although prices, at the time of writing, are beginning to stabilise after the boom of the late 1980s and subsequent recession of the early 1990s, the market is still subject to arbitrary fluctuations.

Restoration

There is a good chance that the weary old thing in your garage is in a worse state than you originally thought so, before you start pulling everything apart, take a deep breath and brace yourself. If you can see a bubble of rust on the outside of the bodywork, rest assured that it will usually be three times as bad on the inside.

Begin by stripping out the interior of the car and storing the seats and interior panels in a safe, dry place along with the windows. If what you see inside the car afterwards is a mass of accumulated filth and grime, take heart from the fact that all of us have on previous occasions.

Cleaning out the mud, dirt, sweet wrappers, 10-pence pieces and old bits of paper is therefore your next job and please don't underestimate how long it will take you. In fact, cleaning everything thoroughly is half the battle in any restoration as well as having the correct tools to hand.

Struggling to loosen nuts and bolts that are caked in oil and mud with a set of molegrips will quickly dampen any enthusiasm for the project you ever had, your old Beetle destined to become an 'abandoned project' along with many hundreds of others for much the same reason.

The next stage is to remove the wings which simply bolt off. If the bolts are firmly encrusted in rust, it pays to spend a few days regularly trickling a good penetrating oil into them but, if time is short, the wings can obviously be cut off with a power chisel. Taking the latter route is extremely quick but won't alleviate the task of removing the bolts. It merely makes them easier to get at and of course, you'll have to invest in a new set of wings afterwards.

It is often the case that all but four of the wing bolts will unscrew easily but those that remain will have to be drilled out and the same applies to the running boards. Never despair and be patient. You will get there in the end.

Having completed these initial stages, discard the old wings, store the light units, label the electric cables, clean up your garage and tools and walk away from the whole thing for a week or longer if you like. Think carefully about what you've done and about what you have to do next.

When you are in the right frame of mind to start again, you will do so in the knowledge that when the garage doors are opened, everything is clean and tidy. Beginning work with a dirty garage floor and having to clear away junk from the last stint will sap your energy and enthusiasm and it is precisely this that forces most people to give up.

At this point, it will be easier to get a better picture of the overall corrosion damage and you will have to decide whether or not the body is to be separated from the chassis. It goes without saying that your decision may be influenced by the available space because obviously, a chassis and a body is going to take up the space of two cars and not one.

Well, think about it for a little while and, in the meantime, remove the engine. For this simple task, you will have to first disconnect the battery and remove it. The engine tinware needs to be unscrewed and removed along with the throttle cable, petrol pipe and flexible heater hoses underneath the car.

For safety's sake, always ensure that the petrol pipe is firmly clamped. In fact, before any welding work begins, it is advisable to drain the fuel system completely, remove the petrol tank and store it as safely away from danger as possible.

Once the four bolts holding the engine to the gearbox are removed, taking the engine out is simple but it is an advantage to have another person available to help you. Despite being made largely of alloy, Beetle engines are heavy and cumbersome for one person to handle.

Before 'dropping' the engine out, I've always found it easiest to support the car at the rear with good sturdy axle stands (never bricks) and to steady the engine out with a trolley jack. If your axle stands are not very tall and the engine proves difficult to draw backwards from under the valance, it's worth removing one of the road wheels to see if it will come sideways. You may have to play about with the engine for quite some time which is where a helping hand is especially useful but rest assured, it will come out in the end.

Fitting a secondhand replacement wing may take some time to achieve a perfect fit but you will get there in the end.

Take a good look around you and clear up the mess. There will be bits and pieces strewn all over the place so label each piece and store it away carefully. If you're new to Beetles, this little operation has probably taken you around two to three hours so, sit down and drink a large quantity of tea. Frequent breaks are essential.

With the engine no longer *in situ,* it is a lot easier to move the car on its wheels if you need to. So, what sort of state is the car in? Scabby round the edges or is it seriously corroded? In the case of the former, you can start cutting out the old rusty metal at the bottom of the doors, front and rear quarter panels and inner wings in readiness for welding in the new panels. Pay particular attention to the sills. Do they really need replacing?

If so, the body ought to be removed. A short cut is welding new sill panels to the chassis, a popular cost-cutting and time-saving move these days but hardly the correct way. If in doubt about the health of the sills, it is better in the long run to go all out and do the job properly so, prepare yourself to remove the body.

Naturally, more bolts will have to be removed along with the steering column. In theory, there is nothing difficult about this exercise save that the body bolts will have almost certainly rusted and their removal, in the usual manner, will take time and patience. But having decided to remove the body, it is imperative to ensure that you take steps to stiffen it up before you do. Most folk brace both sides of the body with steel struts to prevent the metalwork deforming. It can be done with clamps or whatever method you like provided it is taut and can't move.

Volkswagen suspension systems are so durable that for many events, little in the way of modification is needed although a set of Koni shock absorbers will transform the handling.

The result of not doing so will result in a body that will be difficult, if not impossible, to refit on to the floorpan so be warned. Having removed the body and carefully preserved the rubber body belt that seals the unit to the floorpan (consider a replacement by all means), you will have to gather together a few basic tools.

An electric drill, a grinder for cutting out rusty metal and a selection of bodywork hand tools are essential but if you don't want to stretch to the expense of buying a welding machine, you can always hire one when the occasion presents itself.

For welding body panels, it is probably best to stick to MIG welding as it creates less metal distortion when heat is applied. A brand new MIG welder will cost you a few hundred pounds but only the reader can decide whether the outlay is worthwhile.

Local technical colleges frequently run courses on bodywork restoration but are often over-subscribed. If you are unable to join one, enlist the help of your Volkswagen Club. Again, virtually every club has at least one member who will have carried out a major restoration job and all in my experience are only too glad to help.

If you choose to do all the work yourself, it is also worthwhile learning how to do lead-loading, a craftsman's art practised all-too-infrequently nowadays. Plastic body filler has its uses if applied sparingly and for the correct purpose but lead-loading will not only give you a better finish but will last longer as well.

Using molten lead to fill unsightly cracks will cost a good deal more than a tub of plastic body filler but it's very much a case of getting what you pay for. Once again, only the reader is in a position to decide which course is right for him.

And when it comes to cutting out old rusty metal and replacing it with new panels, do one side of the car at a time to prevent the body going horribly out of shape. Normally, it is only the bottom six inches of the car that requires major surgery anyhow because surface corrosion elsewhere can be eradicated later by shotblasting. Good luck and take your time.

After the welding has been satisfactorily completed, the entire shell will have to be prepared for new paint and as any good bodyshop man will tell you, the final result is only ever as good as the preparation. Old paint, if you are doing a bare metal respray can be removed with a powerful stripper such as Nitromors but remember to wear protective clothing and safety glasses at all times when carrying out such a potentially dangerous operation.

Achieving a perfectly finished bodyshell will take a great deal of time but having removed all the paint, time will be against you. Unprotected metal will start going rusty in less than a day which means that base primer coats will have to be applied extremely quickly.

As long as you choose a day that is guaranteed free from interruptions, you needn't worry but get that primer on fast. You can concentrate on flatting down later.

Nowadays, it is preferable to use a good quality two-pack paint for a finish that will not only look well but will also last. However, it is not recommended that you tackle this particular job at home. Two-pack paint gives off a potentially lethal gas and can only be used in conjunction with the correct breathing equipment. A cotton face mask will not suffice so leave the painting of your car to professionals.

Once finished, you can concentrate on rebuilding your car's mechanical components but because you are preparing the car for competition, you have to decide on a specification which complies with the rules for your chosen branch of the sport.

Competition Preparation

The degree to which you prepare your car is dependent on two factors, namely, the amount of money you have to spend and the rules and regulations governing each type of event. It is therefore essential to study 'your' particular sport with great care before rushing out to buy special components which may turn out to be useless.

Most events for which Beetles (and their derivatives) are eligible are controlled by a club which it would be wise to join. It is also essential to obtain a copy of the current RAC 'Blue book' which sets out in full the rules pertaining to all forms of motor sport in Britain. Details can be obtained from the RAC Motor Sports Association Ltd, Motor Sports House, Riverside Park, Colnbrook, Slough SL3 OHG.

When the bodywork is finished, load the car up and send it to a paintshop if you are planning a respray in two-pack. It contains a lethal gas for which special breathing equipment must be used. Do not attempt to spray two-pack at home.

Next, it is necessary to consider your motive for entering a Beetle for competition. Do you want to be ultra competitive, do you merely want to have some fun or perhaps both? The cheapest way to have some fun with a Beetle is in the 'Run what you brung' class in drag racing for which you need only a standard car and a driving licence.

There is no need for a powerful engine, a rollcage or a competition licence but, drive the quarter-mile at Santa Pod and you will soon have the desire to start developing your car into something a little more special.

Drag racing in Britain is broken up into a number of classes and above the 'street' category, there is 'super street' and 'modified'. If your aim is to make a car for either, you will have to consider the extra expense of a crash helmet, fireproof overalls, a rollcage, battery master switch and a good fire extinguisher system.

Take a good look at the highly modified cars such as the ones that belong to Luke Theochari, Keith Seume and John Maher and it will soon become apparent that you're in for some serious expenditure. And it isn't everyone who can take a standard Beetle and turn it into a sub-10 second racer.

Successful drag racers either in super street or modified require hundreds of hours of development before they can even turn a wheel so don't be too ambitious in the first instance.

In the last few years, historic rallying has become one of the fastest growing and

Before deciding upon the engine specification, read the rules and regulations governing your chosen sport very carefully. This 1300 Okrasa unit is ideal for historic rallying but would be no use to someone wanting to take part in the Big Boy's Toys Beetle Cup.

most popular forms of motor sport. There is a bewildering variety of events held throughout the year in both this country and on the European mainland and a number of classes for which Beetles are eligible depending upon the age of your car.

Basically, the Historic Rally Car Register splits cars into two categories; pre-1967 historics and post-historics made after 1967. To join the club and to enter your car, you don't necessarily have to have a genuine historic rally car provided it is of a type that was used on the great rallies of yesteryear.

What the club and its many enthusiastic members are trying to recreate is that which many regard as the golden age of the sport. In other words, there is a large and happy band of lovable eccentrics actively engaged in trying to turn the clock back to the 1950s and '60s and by and large, the cars that form the basis of their enthusiasm are prepared to the same specification as the cars from that era.

For most events, you and your navigator must have a competition licence apiece and a car prepared to fairly stringent rules. As a general rule, it is advisable to take your car to a 'catch all' standard because although a plumbed-in fire extinguisher system is not mandatory for some cars, any self-respecting Beetle owner with a healthy sense of self-preservation ought to fit one. And the same goes for a full rollcage, an internal and external battery cut-out switch and of course, crash helmets are compulsory for stage rallying.

A rollcage, battery cut-out switch, fire-proof overalls, crash helmets and fire extinguishers are also mandatory for rallycross, autocross and circuit racing.

Should you wish to take part in the exciting Beetle Cup series, you will also have to have a competition licence and attend a day's course at one of Britain's many racing schools. In the interest of keeping costs down, the Beetle Cup is governed by strict rules. For example, you may use disc brakes as fitted to the 1500, 1600 GT and 1303S Beetles but all the special competition equipment including the compulsory 1641cc single carburettor engine must be purchased from Beetle specialists Big Boy's Toys.

And whereas the majority of Beetle sports require you to extract more power from the flat-four, lower the suspension and fit rollcages, just the opposite is true of classic reliability and production car trials. For events like the Exeter, Land's End and Edinburgh Trials organised by the Motorcycle Club of Great Britain, it is desirable to raise the ride height of the car and to install a camshaft of a 'non-revving' nature.

Having said that, a number of competitors have done exceptionally well over the years in these events with completely bog-standard cars so, if your idea of fun is driving up formidably steep hills, axle-height in thick mud at low speeds, classic mud-plugging is rewarding, inexpensive and provides a real chance to discover just how tough, dependable and reliable Beetles really are.

And finally, you may like to consider autotesting, said by some to be the quickest way to break a car into its individual components without going to the trouble of driving it off the edge of a cliff. Autotesting is an exceptionally demanding and precise discipline which is designed to examine the ability of both car and driver in a short space of time.

It will take your engine, gearbox and suspension to their limits and beyond if you are sufficiently enthusiastic to want to win so, prepare yourself for time-consuming and often expensive rebuilds.

In the last section of this book, we discussed body restoration and engine removal. It is now, after perusing the various types of competition that we can think about the engine and chassis preparation. Where the Beetle Cup is concerned, you have no choice but to buy a ready-made engine from the organisers of the series so deciding what bits and pieces to use is already done for you.

However for almost all the other events, you have a choice, albeit a limited one in engine size, carburation and the rest. Again, check carefully the regulations governing the types of competition in which you want to participate.

Having already removed the engine, you can consider how to start tuning it. What actually prevents a Beetle engine giving really good performance is its intentionally restricted breathing but merely removing the standard Solex carburettor and replacing it with a dual system won't exactly give you the kick in

Bucket seats with plenty of lateral support are necessary if you are planning to spend most of your time going sideways.

the back you hoped for without carrying out modifications elsewhere.

The use of a 1200 engine as a base from which to start won't do you too many favours either. Ideally, a 1600 twin-port motor provides the most scope for tuning although the 1300 twin-port and 1500 single porters have their uses.

In a nutshell, you will have to polish and port the heads, fit twin Dellorto or Weber carburettors with a suitably modified manifold and a Bosch 009 all-centrifugal distributor and replace the standard exhaust system with one that allows the extra 'punch' you put into the engine to escape more quickly.

A standard camshaft is perfectly acceptable for most jobs but something a little wilder will have to be considered for serious competition but apart from bolting on expensive 'goodies' such as those mentioned above, the essential key to VW tuning is in rebuilding the engine to perfection.

A perfectly balanced crankshaft, pistons and con-rods will improve a standard engine almost beyond recognition and if funds are limited, this is a preferable route to take. Going off on an historic rally with an all-singing and dancing Okrasa unit

A sturdy rollcage is necessary and desirable for most types of competition.

developing zillions of brake horse power is a wonderful experience if you can afford it but a well-built stock engine will allow you to have almost as much fun and the difference in fuel consumption between the two at the end of the day is utterly staggering.

During the 1991 Longleat Stages Rally, Bob Beales's 1958 1300 Okrasa engined car averaged a little more than 7 mpg over the 50-mile course which is surely food for thought for those who hunger for more power. Admittedly, not everyone is able to drive at Beales's customary speed but nevertheless, heavy fuel consumption is the price you have to pay if you want to beat Lotus Cortinas *et al.*

Naturally, the above is a brief beginner's guide to extracting more power but I stress that it is only a start. In addition, you can consider high-lift rockers, an increase in cubic capacity by employing larger barrels and pistons, 16-valve cylinder heads, turbocharging and nitrous oxide injection.

Bear in mind though that the simple expedient of fitting larger barrel and piston kits will probably, depending upon the size you use, require some machining of the heads. A 1500 or 1600 crankcase can be taken out to 1641 or 1679cc without machining but, for 1835cc units and over, you will need to employ the services of a good engine shop.

The greater your tuning ambitions, the more work you will have to do and the more money you will have to spend. Uprating engine power will obviously demand that modifications are made to the lubrication system which means fitting a

The interior of a typical rally car will include stop watches, a Halda tripmaster, additional instrumentation and switches to control the fire extinguisher system and battery cut-out.

stronger oil pump, a separate oil filter, a bolt-on oil tank below the crankcase and even an oil cooler in some instances.

And, after modifying the engine, you will have to consider uprating the brakes and suspension and another limiting factor to blasting off the Porsche fraternity, the gearbox. Now, a standard Beetle gearbox in good condition will withstand an engine developing up to approximately 150 bhp but because of the gearing, your top speed won't even allow you to keep pace with a decent modern family saloon.

Not that top speed matters in rallying, autocross and autotesting but for circuit racing (other than the Beetle Cup where gearbox mods are not permitted) and drag racing at top level, a new gearbox will have to be found.

The highest final drive ratios on standard 'boxes can be found in the 1500, GT and 1600s but for rallying, a powerful engine with a low-ratio 1200 gearbox is ideal. Why not play about with the various combinations and see what suits you best? And in any case, "got the wrong gearbox in" is always a good excuse when you've had one of those off days and nothing seems to be working properly.

A beautiful Okrasa engine like this is a lovely thing to have and to use but will cost you plenty.

If you are on a tight budget, independent Volkswagen specialists always have a useful selection of secondhand spares.

And when you've finally finished your car, use it for the purpose it was intended. It's more fun than you might think. (Photo: Speedsports)

Chassis modifications for most applications can be limited to a set of Koni shock absorbers frankly. Lowering the car for rallying is rarely a good idea although of course, it is essential for circuit racing and for drag racing.

Lowering the rear suspension is a simple matter of turning the torsion bars round a notch or two but at the front, arguably the best method is to fit a Sway-A-Way adjuster, an American device available cheaply through independent specialists.

To fit a Sway-A-Way, you must remove the front torsion beam from the framehead and relieve it of both its torsion leaves and trailing arms. The beam then must be cut in two and the adjusters welded in. A full set of instructions comes with each set. After putting everything back together again, the ride height can be adjusted by unscrewing the locking nuts on the adjusters with a special Allen key.

Many of the top drag racing cars dispense with conventional Beetle suspension altogether and utilize simple dampers and coil springs in the interest of saving weight. Also to save weight, glass fibre is used extensively for the bodywork and in some cases, the platform chassis is even dispensed with in favour of a tubular frame unit.

The number of permutations and combinations of engine/gearbox/chassis/ bodywork is almost never ending. There are literally thousands but, all said and done, tuning can only make a difference to the results sheet up to a point. History has shown us time and again that the person behind the wheel can make the biggest difference to the performance of a motor car and to Beetles in particular.

Time and again, enthusiasm and determination in the cockpit has won through against superior power. Look after your Beetle, learn how to get the most from it by constant practice and it will reward you richly. Bill Bengry has shown us all exactly what can be done with a Beetle seemingly against the odds. Now well into his 70s, Bill has owned and still owns a wide variety of cars. His Herefordshire garage deals in Peugeots these days, cars which Bill holds in high regard but when I asked him recently what sort of car would be his first choice for a trip from England to South Africa, he unhesitatingly replied, "A Beetle".

When asked why, Bill said in his wonderful Herefordshire accent, "Because it's the only bloody car I know that would guarantee to get me there in one piece." And Bill should know because there aren't many countries in the world where he has not driven one type of car or another.

Buying A Brand New Beetle

Rebuilding and restoring a Beetle for either the road or track is a most rewarding, if sometimes painful experience but for those who have neither the time, nor skill to spend months on end in a freezing cold garage cutting out rusty metal and trying to weld in new panels, there is a swift and pleasurable alternative . . . buying a brand new Beetle.

As the Volkswagen plant in Mexico continues to make Beetles today at a rate of around 500 units per day, it is possible to acquire one despite the fact that they are not officially imported to Europe by the parent German company.

However, buying a car from Mexico is a little more complicated than nipping down to your local dealer and signing a piece of paper. The first step is to contact a Mexican dealer who has already supplied Beetles to people living in the United Kingdom. One such is Senor Octavio A Lozano Gamez based in Nuevo Laredo (full details can be found at the end of this book) who also speaks fluent English.

Nuevo Laredo is on the Mexican side of the border opposite Laredo, Texas, so collecting a car from the dealership means a short journey into Mexico from the USA. It is not difficult to travel to southern Texas, cross the border into Nuevo Laredo from Laredo, collect the car, complete the paperwork and other formalities and return to the USA.

It is important to transfer the money to the dealer's account and the dealer will probably require full payment in US dollars upon accepting an order for a car. At the time of writing, the account of the above dealer is as follows; Bancomer, Nuevo Laredo, Tamaulipas, Mexico; account Automotriz Lor SA de CV; number 14666-6.

Depending upon the delay between payment and collection of the car, arrange for the sales invoice to be sent to your home address or to be kept at the dealership and collected at the same time as the car.

By far the best way of getting to Mexico is to take a flight to an airport on the east coast of America and then catch a bus or a plane to Texas. It is possible to fly to San Antonio, Texas and take a Greyhound bus to Laredo. Laredo is 150 miles from San Antonio and the bus takes about three hours. It isn't possible to get off the bus at Nuevo Laredo as the next stop is Monterey. Cross from Laredo to Nuevo Laredo on foot or by taxi.

Before starting the trip, it is essential to obtain a US visa and a copy of the USA customs document 'Importing a Car' available from the Department of Treasury, US Customs Service, Washington DC 20229. Traveller's cheques, a current driving licence, medical insurance and a note of your national insurance number are also essential documents you should keep with you at all times.

For between £6-7,000, you can buy a brand new Beetle from Mexico and have a good holiday into the bargain.

Once on US soil, it is important to obtain insurance to cover against an accident, fire, theft and the other normal risks. The American Automobile Association at 7100 North San Bernardo, Laredo, Texas is probably your best bet for insurance cover or alternatively, a Laredo broker. Mexican registered cars require their owners to give a Mexican address when applying for insurance so, you will be asked not only for the address of your hotel but probably your British home address as well. In the past, it has also been normal practice to give the dealer's address at Nuevo Laredo as a local address for the duration of the trip.

Once back in the USA with your new car, you have to drive to a port for shipping the car back home across the Atlantic. Port Elizabeth in New Jersey and Portsmouth, Virginia are the most popular. The shipping line, Wallenius Motorships Inc operates in both New Jersey and Virginia and sails to Liverpool and Southampton. Wallenius can be contacted at 482 Hudson Terrace, PO Box 1157, Englewood Cliffs, New Jersey 07632, Telephone (from UK) 0101-201 871 0700.

Cars are shipped unboxed and will cost you less than £500 payable in US dollars before the journey or in sterling upon collection in Britain. Marine insurance is advisable and will add less than £100 to the overall cost. After you fly home and await the arrival of your new Beetle, you will have to collect together a number of documents which include proof of your identity, dealer's invoice, completed Customs form C386, Mexican vehicle registration document, completed GSP

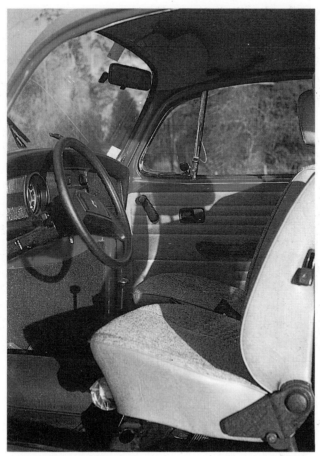

The Mexican Beetle's interior has reclining seats, a padded dashboard and is very modern indeed.

certificate and the duty payable, by banker's draft, building society cheque or even cash. For details of the duty payable on importing the car, write to H.M. Customs and Excise, Vehicle Appraisal Unit, Parcel Post Depot, Charlton Green, Dover, Kent CT16 1BH. Tell the unit that you are importing a used 1600cc Mexican Beetle giving the year of manufacture and that you intend it for you own personal use. Give an estimate of the mileage that the car will have travelled from the dealership to the shipping port. A personal import has to be owned, registered and used overseas before being imported and registered in the UK for personal use.

After obtaining customs clearance, go to the offices of Mann Motorships, pay the shipping, freight, insurance and wharfage charges and inspect the car. If it's alright, obtain a port exit permit and enjoy driving your new Beetle home.

The overall cost of your new car obviously varies. Your trip to Mexico will obviously increase in cost if you stay at expensive hotels but between £6 – 7,000 should be sufficient not only to buy your new car but to have a good holiday at the same time.

The 1600cc engines of today's south American Beetles are fitted with catalytic converters and run on a full-time diet of unleaded petrol. Note there is only one tailpipe and not two.

If you are thinking about buying a new Beetle in Mexico, it is important to check on the above information in greater detail by contacting Howard Cheese of the British-based Mexican/Brazilian Beetle Register. Howard is a mine of up-to-date information and has experienced importing a Beetle from Mexico for himself. His address also appears at the end of this book.

Volkswagen Beetle 1600 1993 Model Year Specification

The current Volkswagen Beetle is built by Volkswagen de Mexico SA de CV in Puebla, Mexico and has been in continuous production there since 1964. Although other Volkswagens are built at the plant, the Beetle is by far the best-selling model in Mexico and, there are no plans to discontinue production in the foreseeable future as is often thought to be the case.

Mexican Beetles are mechanically and bodily similar to those produced in Germany in the 1978 model year when production in that country ceased for good. However, the south American cars have been brought up to date and boast many features, such as a catalytic converter, that you would expect to find on any modern motor car.

Engine

ACD series twin-port 1,584cc horizontally opposed air-cooled four cylinder petrol engine with multi-point Digifant fuel-injection producing 60 bhp at a max 4,000 rpm. To allow the use of low-octane fuels, the compression ratio is 6.6:1 and the piston crowns are recessed. A three-way catalytic converter with lambda probe is now fitted to the exhaust system which has a single tail pipe. The engine runs on a full-time diet of unleaded petrol.

Brakes

Dual-circuit split diagonally, hydraulic brakes with drums all round.

Lighting

Headlamps are plastic lensed halogen H4 units without sidelight bulbs. Amber indicator units in front bumper contain double-filament lamp. A lamp is attached to the inside of the engine lid which can be illuminated manually with a switch that is attached to it.

Interior

Front seats are fully reclining covered with a hard-wearing cloth and fitted with adjustable head-restraints. Full headlining. Front seat belts are inertia reel type, rear belts are lap type. Rear seat tilts forward to give additional luggage space. A rear parcel shelf is not fitted. There are no heater outlets under the rear seat as on German Beetles. Warning triangle and tool kit are provided as standard equipment. Fire extinguisher under driver's seat. A dipping rear-view mirror is attached to the windscreen. Smoker's companion fitted front and rear. Dashboard is padded *a la* GT Beetle and 1303 German cars. No radio fitted as standard. Dual circuit brake warning lamp. The 160 Km speedometer features a fuel gauge and warning lamps for generator, oil pressure, indicators and headlamp main beam in addition to its prime function.

Windscreen wipers are two-speed plus intermittent. When windscreen washer activated, wipers automatically give four full sweeps. Screen washer powered by electric pump. Active charcoal filter which absorbs petrol vapour from fuel tank.

Suspension

Torsion-bar springing all round but with double-jointed rear axles.

Exterior

Steel chromium-plated front bumper has integral indicator units, $4^1/_2$J steel road wheels shod with 155x15 radial tyres, wheel nut caps and centre nut caps in black plastic. Chromed exterior mirror on driver's (left) side. Engine lid lock. Rear valance is extended type with single tail-pipe cutout. Anodised trim on side windows only. Laminated windscreen.

Bonnet and engine lid rubber seals now fitted to the lids and not to the bodywork as previously. Four banks of cooling louvres on engine lid. No underseal under wings or floorpan.

Colours

Alpine White, Tornado Red, Amarillo Yellow, Cosmos Blue. Also at extra cost to celebrate the production of the 21 millionth Beetle, Light Blue Metallic, Turkish Green Metallic and Grey Metallic.

Options

Radio with aerial, rear parcel shelf incorporating two loud speakers, VW sports mats, alarm system, quarter-light window locks, rubber overriders, jump leads, leatherette steering wheel cover, rear mud flaps, spot lamps, sports steering wheel, tunnel tray incorporating drinks holder, glovebox lock, front boot lock, toolbox, front parcel shelf, sports exhaust system, sports shock absorbers, wider tyres, sports front seats.

NB   To comply with English law, a fog lamp must be fitted to the rear offside of the vehicle, Headlamps must be changed to UK specification which dip to the correct side and have glass lenses.

Beetles Made In Britain

An alternative to both restoring a Beetle or buying one from Mexico is to have one tailor made. Peter Stevens's company, Autobarn based in Pershore, Worcestershire specialises in constructing new Beetles by hand from brand new parts shipped from Mexico and Germany.

A brand new Beetle made in Pershore, England by Autobarn. These cars are assembled largely by hand using parts from Germany and Mexico. Built to an extremely high standard, each car costs around £18,000 depending upon the specification ordered.

Peter spent two years designing a special body jig prior to opening his firm and although Autobarn Beetles aren't cheap at around £18,000 each, they are superbly made and use only genuine Volkswagen parts throughout.

The cars are made to order and to the latest Mexican specification although twin carburettors for example, can be fitted instead of fuel injection. Better equipped

Autobarn's managing director, Peter Stevens, who spent two years designing a special body jig on which to make his cars.

for the '90s than their illustrious forbears from Germany, Autobarn Beetles can be specified with partially galvanised bodyshells, sports wheels and tinted windows to name but a few touches that set them aside from the Mexican-built cars.

"We set out to make the same sort of car that the factory in Wolfsburg would had it continued making Beetles today," says Peter. To that end, his Beetles are fitted with catalytic converters, side-impact beam in the doors and a host of other safety-related features.

They are also finished to an amazingly high standard with perfect panel fit and paint quality. Full details are available from Peter Stevens on (0386)710710.

Useful Names And Addresses

Howard Cheese, Mexican/Brazilian Volkswagen Register
The Hoopits, Greete, Near Ludlow, Shropshire.

Senor Octavio A Lozano Gamez, Director General, Automotriz Lor SA de CV,
Concesionario Autorizado Volkswagen, Carretera Laredo-Monterrey, Km 7,
Apdo. Postal 130, CP 88000 Nuevo Laredo, Tamaulipas, Mexico.

Telephone (from UK): 010 52 871 40600
    Fax (from UK): 010 52 871 51600.

Beetles Revival Fahrzeughandel und Karosseriebau,
Fliederweg 11, 0-2801, Wobbelin, Germany (east).
Importers of Mexican Beetles to Germany.

Telephone (from UK): 010 49 161 340 6030 (mobile)
                      between 10.00-13.00 Mon-Fri GMT
    Fax (from UK): 010 49 721 681 255
                    24 hours.

Mrs Alison Woolley, The Historic Rally Car Register
Tibberton Court, Tibberton, Gloucester GL19 3AF.

The RAC Motor Sports Association Limited
Motor Sports House, Riverside Park, Colnbrook, Slough SL3 0HG.

G. Thomas, VW Drag Racing Club
15 St Cross Road, Crondall, Farnham, Surrey GU10 5PQ.

Shaun Hollamby, Big Boys' Toys
Unit 1, Motherwell Way, West Thurrock, Grays, Essex RM16 1NR,

Geoffrey Margetts, Motorcycle Club of Great Britain
21 Madresfield Road, Malvern, Worcestershire WR14 2AS.

Peter Stevens, Autobarn Beetles
Manor Farm House, Kersoe, near Pershore, Worcestershire, Telephone (0386)
710710.

Volkswagen Owners Club of Great Britain
71 Hamble Drive, Abingdon, Oxfordshire OX14 3TF.

V.A.G. (United Kingdom)Ltd
Yeomans Drive, Blakelands, Milton Keynes MK14 5AN,

Volkswagen AG
3180 Wolfsburg 1, Germany.

Specialist Volkswagen Magazines

VolksWorld
Link House, Dingwall Avenue, Croydon, Surrey CR9 2TA.

VW Motoring
Stoke Orchard, Cheltenham, Gloucestershire GL52 4SX.

Volkswagen Audi Car
Market Chambers, High Street, Toddington, Bedfordshire, LU5 6BY.

Hot VWs
PO Box 2260, Costa Mesa, California 92628.

Gute Fahrt
Gutenbergstrasse 13, 7302 Ostfildern 4, Germany.

International Vintage VW Magazine
194 Old Church Road, St. Leonard's-on-Sea, East Sussex TN38 9HD.